Late Antique
and Early Christian
Book Illumination

Late Antique and Early Christian Book Illumination

Kurt Weitzmann

Chatto & Windus   London

First published in the UK in 1977 by
Chatto & Windus Ltd., London

ISBN 0 7011 2243 9

Printed and bound in West Germany by Mohndruck, Gütersloh

Acknowledgements

The author and the publisher would like to express their sincere thanks to the following institutions and individuals who kindly provided materials and granted permission to reproduce them in this volume.

Color Plates

BERLIN, Deutsche Staatsbibliothek Berlin/DDR, Plate 5.

CAMBRIDGE, Master and Fellows of Corpus Christi College, Plates 41, 42.

FLORENCE, Biblioteca Mediceo Laurenziana, Plates 34, 35, 36, 37, 38, 48 (Photo, Guido Sansoni, Florence).

LONDON, The British Library (by permission of the British Library Board), Plates 21, 22, 43.

LONDON, The Egypt Exploration Society, Plate 6 (Photo, University College, London).

MILAN, Biblioteca Ambrosiana, Plates 7, 8, 9, 10.

PARIS, Bibliothèque Nationale, Plates 39, 40, 44, 45, 46, 47 (Photo, Bibl. Nat. Paris).

ROME, Vatican City, Biblioteca Apostolica Vaticana, Plates 1, 2, 3, 4, 11, 12, 13, 14 (Photo, Biblioteca Vaticana).

VIENNA, Österreichische Nationalbibliothek, Plates 15, 16, 17, 18, 19, 20, 23, 24, 25, 26, 27, 28.

WASHINGTON, D.C., Dumbarton Oaks, W. C. Loerke, Plates 29, 30, 31, 32, 33 (Photo, Carlo Bertelli, Gabinetto Fotographico, Rome).

Black-and-White Figures

FLORENCE, Biblioteca Mediceo Laurenziana, Figure XVII.

LONDON, The Egypt Exploration Society, Figure II (Photo courtesy the Ashmolean Museum, Oxford).

MUNICH, Hirmer Fotoarchiv, Figure XV.

PARIS, Bibliothèque Nationale, Figures I, XI, XII, XIII, XIV (Photo, Bibl. Nat. Paris).

ROME, Vatican City, Biblioteca Apostolica Vaticana, Figures III, IV, V, VI, VIII, IX, X (Photo, Biblioteca Vaticana).

VIENNA, Österreichische Nationalbibliothek, Figure VII (Photo, Lichtbildwerkstätte Alpenland, Vienna).

WASHINGTON, D.C., Dumbarton Oaks, W. C. Loerke, Frontispiece, Figure XVI.

Contents

Introduction 9

Selected Bibliography 25

Descriptions of Manuscripts 27

Color Plates and Commentaries 32

Introduction

I

One of the most important events in the history of the book, comparable in impact to Gutenberg's invention of printing, was the introduction of the codex (in the form in which it is still used today) at the end of the first century A.D. The poet Martial wrote several epigrams (XIV, 186, 192, etc.) in praise of the new "book with many folded skins" which made it possible to have the whole of Vergil's writings in one volume. Previously books were made in the form of papyrus rolls, on an average 30–35 feet in length; the twelve books of the *Aeneid* had to be written on as many scrolls. For several centuries roll and codex competed with each other, and not before the fourth century did the codex become the predominant form.

The Egyptians had written their Book of the Dead on papyrus, a material native to their country and on which they had a monopoly. Not before Alexander's conquest of Egypt and the foundation of Alexandria did papyrus become widespread in the Greek, and later in the Roman, world. When the Museion, the famous library of Alexandria, burned at the time of Julius Caesar it possessed 700,000 scrolls, if we can believe the sources. Many of these must have been illustrated, and the loss for literature and for illumination must be considered equally tragic.

What, then, is our evidence that scrolls were illustrated? There is a famous passage in Pliny (*Naturalis Historia* XXXV.II.11) recounting that Varro (first century B.C.) "inserted in a prolific output of volumes portraits of seven hundred famous people" and adding that these were spread all over the world. This suggests the mass production of ambitiously illustrated literary texts and an active market for them in pre-Christian times. It can be taken for granted that all kinds of natural science texts were illustrated by explanatory pictures. Here again, Pliny is our best witness (*N. H.* XXV.IV.8), telling us that the herbals of Crateuas, Dionysius, and Metrodorus were "most attractively" illustrated with colored like-

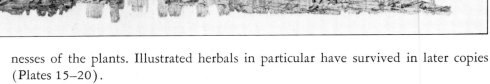

nesses of the plants. Illustrated herbals in particular have survived in later copies (Plates 15–20).

Because of the perishability of papyrus and the loss of the libraries of Alexandria, it cannot come as a surprise that so little remains of papyrus illustration. Among the few surviving papyrus fragments of literary texts are those of a romance from the second century, in Paris (Figure I), and another of a Heracles poem from the third century, in London (Figure II). The method of illustrating such literary texts was quite consistent: the illustrator rendered as many events as possible in concise, frameless scenes which follow each other in quick succession so that the beholder is induced to move from one to the next. This general principle survived in many codices (Figure X) and is still widely used in modern times in the comic strip.

The codex opened new possibilities. Flat parchment sheets, not having to be rolled like papyrus, permitted the application of thicker layers of paint. This offered the possibility of copying pictorially those more advanced panel and fresco paintings with which miniature painting soon competed in refinement of coloration. Moreover, the codex page invited the isolation and enlargement of a single scene and thus the imitation of the general effect of an actual panel, fresco, or mosaic (Plates 30–31, 36–38). As a result, miniature painting achieved a high artistic level in the fourth century and soon became a leading art form, a position it held until the miniature was replaced by the woodcut and engraving.

It must, however, be emphasized that, since so few Late Antique and Early Christian manuscripts and fragments (roughly from the fourth to the seventh century) have come down to us, a coherent history cannot be written. Even the few manuscripts which can be taken as reliable copies of lost, datable models (Figures IV–VI, VIII–X) do not suffice to fill the gaps in what might justifiably be called the first golden age of book illumination.

III

The most common form of illustration in all types of texts was the author portrait. In the papyrus roll, the evidence points to this having been, as a rule, a medallion portrait. Such a medallion is reflected in the author portrait in the Vatican Terence manuscript (Figure VIII), where the codex format has made possible its enlargement and elaboration by the addition of two flanking actors. In the codex, the seated author became the most widely accepted form of author portrait. In initial stages, as in the *Vergilius Romanus* (Figure III), he is still squeezed into a narrow strip within a writing column, the empty space on either side being filled with a pulpit and a *capsa*, the box to contain the scrolls. The final solution came in the full-page author portrait, such as that of Dioscurides (Plate 17), who sits in front of a colonnaded building. Classical poets and philosophers became models for the portraits of the Evangelists, the most frequently depicted authors in the long history of book illumination (Plates 33, 35, 42), and here colonnaded buildings, in some cases clearly derived from the *scenae frons* of the Roman theater (Plate 33), are a common feature.

The earliest dated codex with full-page illustrations is, unfortunately, preserved only in seventeenth-century drawings based on an intermediary Carolingian copy. The Calendar of Filocalus of 354 A.D., made for a Christian by the name of Valentinus, reveals both the complexity of the sources used by the first illustrators of full-page miniatures, and their high artistic standards. The Emperor Constans II, enthroned and distributing coins (Figure IV), is a subject found on silver plates; personifications of the great metropolitan cities, like *Roma* (Figure V), have parallels in frescoes; and the series of the Occupations of the Months, depicted by full-length figures (Figure VI), is most familiar in contemporary floor mosaics.

It is characteristic of Late Antique book illumination that texts of practical value, such as the calendar and some scientific texts, were illustrated on the same high artistic level as famed literary texts. Some of the most refined miniatures we

IV

V

VI

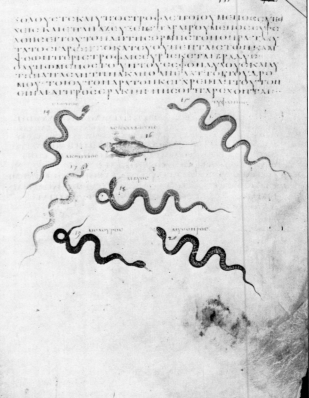

VII

have from that period are in an herbal manuscript made in Constantinople for an imperial princess. This Dioscurides manuscript in Vienna, in addition to sumptuous title miniatures (Plates 15–17), has not only delicately painted plant pictures of great verisimilitude (Plate 18), but also very naturalistic pictures to appended treatises: one to a poem on the healing powers of plants, with an elaborate picture of a coral (Plate 19), another to a treatise on birds (Plate 20), and a third on the poisonous bites of serpents (Figure VII).

Among the literary texts of antiquity, epic poems had the greatest popularity, and foremost among these were Homer's *Iliad* and *Odyssey*. From about the end of the fifth century we have a set of fifty-eight miniatures cut out of an *Iliad* now in Milan (Plates 7–10) which show a considerable diversity of compositional schemes, from single combat to complex battle scenes. This indicates that, by that time, *Iliad* illustration had passed through various stages of development and thus had a long history behind it. It seems mere chance that neither an illustrated *Odyssey* nor any of the other Greek epic poems has survived.

From the Latin West two illustrated manuscripts of Vergil's *Aeneid* have come down to us, both in the Vatican Library: the *Vergilius Vaticanus*, attributed to the early, and the *Vergilius Romanus* to the later fifth century (Plates 1–4, 11–14). Not only are they totally different in style, one having been made in Rome and the other in an undetermined province, but they are also different in their iconography, suggesting that illustration of the *Aeneid* began in more than one place.

Next in popularity among illustrated literary texts were the dramas. Unfortunately none has survived from Late Antiquity, but a Carolingian manuscript of the comedies of Terence in the Vatican must be considered a most faithful copy of a fifth-century model, associated with a new edition of the comedies by a certain Calliopius. The illustrations are laid out in a manner which must have characterized all illustrated dramas: first comes the author portrait (Figure VIII), then the catalogue of the masks in their exact shapes and proper colors (Figure IX), and then the lively narrative scenes within the text columns, without frame or background, still continuing the papyrus tradition (Figure X). Illustrated manuscripts of Euripides and Menander, the most popular classical dramatists, must have looked quite similar.

Both Vergil manuscripts mentioned above also contain the *Georgics*, with a variety of miniatures of occupations and animal lore (Plates 1, 12), and the *Vergilius Romanus* has some of the *Eclogues* (Plate 11), depicting the happy pastoral life which, through bucolic literature, had spread widely and deeply influenced Christian art. An illustrated Theocritus manuscript may well have been the first bucolic text to be illustrated. The second-century papyrus in Paris, with scenes from an unidentified romance (Figure I), suggests that this category of texts must also have existed, and included extensive miniature cycles.

To get a true perspective on emerging Early Christian book illumination, one must constantly keep in mind the vastness of ancient book illumination with its tradition of several centuries. Early Christian book illumination was not a new branch of art, but made from the start a strong effort to absorb the classical tradition, not only by following the technical aspects of classical books, but also by adapting their prevailing style, their compositional schemes wherever this was possible, and, in general, their system of extensive, narrative picture cycles.

TERENTI

VIII

IX

X

In the center of Early Christian book illumination stands the Bible, assuming a position comparable to that of Homer in ancient book illumination. It is most significant that the illustration started not with the whole, but with individual books of the Bible, for the obvious reason that the scenes follow in such quick succession and are so numerous that, on this scale, the illustration of the entire Bible would have been a practical impossibility.

Our earliest Biblical miniatures—four in number—are from a luxuriously illustrated Books of Kings manuscript in Berlin, the so-called *Quedlinburg Itala* from the early fifth century (Plate 5). Several scenes fill each page, and calculating that the original codex had perhaps sixty such illustrated pages, it would have had two hundred or three hundred individual scenes. As illustrations from Kings they are without parallel, and yet the fact that narrative illustrations from Kings comprise a major part of the wall decoration in the fresco cycle of the synagogue of Dura from the third century suggests the existence of an older picture tradition for this book of the Old Testament.

The best evidence of extensive miniature cycles exists for the Book of Genesis, which, judging from the fact that there existed several picture recensions, must have enjoyed special popularity with its many dramatic episodes, so attractive to illustrators. The very nature of early Bible illustration is best revealed by the so-called Cotton Genesis in London from the fifth or sixth century (Plates 21–22), which, unfortunately, burned in 1731. Yet charred fragments still remain of the majority of its original 330 or so miniatures, which give an insight into the mentality of the artist, who tried to illustrate a single episode in as many successive scenes as possible. The ark of Noah, for example, appeared no fewer than eleven times and in the genealogical chapter there appeared, somewhat monoto-

XI

nously, one birth scene after another. The manuscript was highly appreciated throughout its history. In the thirteenth century, mosaicists in Venice chose about a hundred of its scenes as models for the decorations of five cupolas in the entrance hall of San Marco; and in the seventeenth century, one of the greatest scholars of his time, Peiresc, had planned a facsimile edition with engravings which, had it materialized, would have been the earliest manuscript facsimile. Unfortunately, only two preparatory drawings for the engravings are left of this project, one of which depicts the third day of Creation (Figure XI).

To a Genesis manuscript of even greater splendor belongs a series of twenty-four folios with forty-eight miniatures from the sixth century, now in the Vienna Library, and known as the Vienna Genesis (Plates 23–28). It has been calculated that the original manuscript had ninety-six folios (i.e., 192 pages), each of which had a miniature in its lower half, while the upper half contained the text, written in silver uncial on purple-stained parchment. Since the average miniature has two or three scenes, the original number of scenes here even surpasses that of the Cotton Genesis. The manuscript must have been made for a bibliophile (perhaps a member of the imperial family) who was interested more in the pictures than in the text, which was considerably shortened in order to adjust it to the balance of text and miniatures on each page. Manuscripts of this kind were a rarity at all times and appreciated as such. The Vienna Genesis also inspired later artists, in this case, a Venetian miniaturist of the fourteenth century who illustrated a *Historia Troiana*.

Larger groups of illustrated biblical books were the Octateuch in the Greek East, of which only later copies have come down to us, and the Pentateuch in the Latin West, of which one early, luxuriously illustrated copy has survived, the seventh-century Ashburnham Pentateuch in Paris (Plates 44–47). Again, one can only marvel at the extensiveness of its illustration. The original number of full-page miniatures with scenic illustration has been estimated at sixty-nine, of which only eighteen are left, and because of the large size of the folios (ca. 40 cm. in height), the illustrator in many cases was able to collect more individual scenes on a page than in the Vienna Genesis; surely the scenes in the Ashburnham Pentateuch also must be counted by the hundreds. Typically, more·than half of them illustrated Genesis, but iconographically they are unrelated to the previously discussed Genesis cycles. The Ashburnham Pentateuch was also highly appreciated in the Middle Ages, some of its pictures being used as models for the eleventh-century frescoes of the church of St. Julian in Tours.

The problems which faced the artist coping with the illustration of a full Bible become apparent in a Syriac Bible of the seventh century, now in Paris. There are only title miniatures to individual books of this Bible whose text, for reasons of economy, is written in three columns. In most cases the illustrations consist of standing author figures, like Sirach in front of a colonnade (Figure XII) or the scene of Joshua at Gibeon turned into a title figure (Figure XIII), while only in a few cases, as for Exodus and Job, were more elaborate narrative scenes excerpted from larger cycles (Plates 39–40). The lack of any consistent principle clearly reveals the eclectic nature of this system of illustration.

A very special position is taken by the Gospel Book. There is evidence that its illustration began in a manner similar to that of the Old Testament—with extensive cycles of miniatures within the text columns, so dense that no event of Christ's life was omitted. Two such Gospel Books with hundreds of scenes, both copies from the eleventh century, one now in Paris and the other in Florence, reflect this system of illustration. Apparently not very long after the firm establishment of the Christian Church, Gospel Books were produced not to be kept on the library shelf, but to be deposited on the altar table, as the focal point of the service. Such Gospel Books, splendid and of stately size—and all extant early illustrated Gospels belong to this category—have at the top of the pages the title of the lection and the indication of the day when it was read, to facilitate the Gospel's practical use. Perhaps not to distract the Gospel reader, at an early stage of development the pictures were taken out of the writing column and placed either in the margin or collected at the beginnings of the individual Gospels or the whole Gospel Book. Among the few illustrated Gospel Books or fragments thereof, all three systems occur.

A sixth-century Gospel fragment from Sinope, containing part of Saint Matthew's Gospel and written in huge golden uncial script on purple parchment, has all five remaining illustrations in the lower margin. They are flanked by prophets who hold scrolls with typological texts. Such a scene as Christ talking to the withering fig tree (Figure XIV), which is not of primary importance, suggests that the illustrator chose from a larger repertory of narrative Gospel scenes.

In the closely related Gospel Book in the Cathedral treasure of Rossano, written in silver uncial on purple parchment and likewise belonging to the sixth century, all illustrations are gathered at the beginning of the Gospel Book. The sub-

jects were chosen to illustrate important readings. Here, in the splendid full-page miniatures, the illustrator was apparently inspired by monumental art, both fresco and mosaic. This applies not only to the huge pictures of Christ before Pilate (Plates 30–31), but also to the Communion of the Apostles (Figures XV–XVI), which he spread across the tops of two facing pages, as well as of all the smaller scenes, which ultimately go back to a narrative cycle of illustrations but, in combination with the Prophets underneath, reflect the organization of a wall decoration such as that of the church of Sant' Angelo in Formis.

A different system was used in the Syriac Gospel Book in Florence, which was written by the monk Rabbula in Mesopotamia in 586 A.D. Here a narrative Gospel cycle from the Annunciation to Zaccharias to Christ before Pilate, is placed in the inner and outer margins of the Canon Tables (Plate 34) preceding the Gospel text, while Prophets, derived from an illustrated Bible such as the Syriac manuscript in Paris (Figure XII), fill the spandrels. In addition, the four Evangelists, usually full-page miniatures, are integrated into the Canon Tables (Plate 35). But then, as in the Rossano Gospels, there are also very sumptuous full-page miniatures which have the characteristics of monumental art (Plates 36–38). One has the impression that in the Early Christian period the various media—miniatures, frescoes and perhaps also icons—influenced each other freely.

The Latin West also adapted the system of collecting the narrative cycle on separate pages, as in the Corpus Christi College Gospels in Cambridge from the end of the sixth century. Heading at least three of the Gospels were collective

miniatures, one of which remains (Plate 41). Essentially, the scenes in this miniature are of a narrative character, illustrating the first half of the Passion. For
additional scenes the artists placed very condensed double scenes left and right
of the Evangelist picture (Plate 42), an arrangement comparable to the New
Testament scenes flanking the Canon Tables of the Rabbula Gospels (Plate 34).

The Gospel Book assumes a special place in early book illustration as the only
book which had a rich ornamental decoration. It must almost be a surprise, seen
from the point of view of later development, that the early books, particularly
those produced in the Mediterranean, are rather bare of the ornament such as
developed in northern European Merovingian and Insular art. There is one excep-
tion, and that is in the Canon Tables preceding the Gospel Book, which contain
the concordance of Gospel passages as worked out in the fourth century by
Eusebius. A full set of no fewer than nineteen tables for the ten canons precedes
the Rabbula Gospels (Plate 34), where an arch, which occurs also as a frame
for the Evangelist portraits (Plate 33), is used as a basic motif. It is largely de-
prived of its architectural function and often, as in the Rabbula Canon Tables, is
filled with abstract and floral decorations, and crowned by flowers and birds. Fragments of four Greek Canon Tables in London show the height of ornamental
richness and exuberance (Plate 43). In the Rossano Gospels there is, in addition,
a frontispiece to the Canon Tables with a wreath composed of rainbow-colored
disks and incorporating the medallions of the four Evangelists (Frontispiece).
Moreover, in some Gospel Books, the Canon Tables are followed by a picture of

the so-called Fountain of Life of which, however, only ninth-century and later copies are preserved. It is also important to record that, in the East, the Gospel Book is the only, and in the West, the principal, book decorated with golden, jewel, and pearl-studded covers, sometimes with the addition of ivory and enamel, thus enhancing its appearance as a cult object comparable to the chalice and paten.

To try to write a coherent stylistic history of Late Antique and Early Christian book illumination would be futile, since all that is left is comparable to a few islands in an ocean reaching farther than the eye can see. *A priori* one can assume that the main creative centers for both the Late Antique and the Early Christian luxury codices were the great traditional metropolitan centers which had become the seats of the early patriarchates: Rome, Alexandria, Antioch, and Constantinople. To these centers and their orbits one should try to attribute as many as possible of the extant manuscripts. Yet some attributions are inevitably hypothetical, and for other manuscripts the place of origin remains completely elusive.

With the earliest manuscripts we are, fortunately, on sure ground. There is general agreement that the *Vergilius Vaticanus* (Plates 1–4) and the *Quedlinburg Itala* (Plate 5) were produced in Rome, not impossibly in the same scriptorium, thus being a striking example of a parallel development in classical and Christian book production of an equally high quality. Their miniatures are steeped in an illusionistic tradition, particularly evident in the rich landscape settings, apparently adapted from fresco painting or mosaics such as those of the contemporary Old Testament panels in the nave of Santa Maria Maggiore.

To Alexandria has generally been ascribed the Cotton Genesis (Plates 21–22). In Alexandria an impressionistic style was rampant in the Hellenistic and Roman periods, but of this not much is left in the Genesis miniatures. The figures are thickset, with straight outlines, set into boxlike architecture, obviously reflecting the impact of the Egyptian hinterland where art forms of the older Egyptian tradition had survived in the Early Christian period and had been reinforced after the Council of Chalcedon in 451 A.D., when the monophysite church split from the orthodoxy centered in Constantinople. A closely related papyrus fragment found at Antinoë (Plate 6) supports the attribution of the Genesis to Egypt. The attribution of the Milan *Iliad* to Alexandria is not undisputed, since Constantinople has also been proposed as a place of origin. Yet the style of the figures with their straight outlines (Plate 8) has much in common with that of the Cotton Genesis,

XVI

whereas Constantinople in the sixth century had preserved a much more classical style.

To the Eastern capital can be ascribed with certainty the Vienna Dioscurides, roughly contemporary with the Milan *Iliad* and the Cotton Genesis. In particular, the miniature with the author portrait (Plate 17) shows a purity of the classical tradition that occurs in no other Mediterranean center in the sixth century, and one can only conclude that Constantinople, being of Greek foundation, had taken special pride in preserving the Hellenistic heritage. To Constantinople have also been ascribed the fragments of the Greek Canon Tables (Plate 43), demonstrating that, at least in ornament, Constantinople was open to influences from the Orient and able to render ornamental features of unsurpassed quality.

The three purple manuscripts, the Vienna Genesis, the Rossano, and the Sinope Gospels (Plates 23–33, Figure XIV), form a coherent group which, because of the purple which was an imperial prerogative, had been ascribed by some scholars to Constantinople. Yet the style is quite different from that of the author pictures in the Vienna Dioscurides. The figures in the purple manuscripts are tubular and often swaying, the backs of the heads exaggerated (e.g. Plate 29), and the faces oriental-looking. There is a deviation from the classical figure type which points to the influence of a hinterland with a distinct style. We believe this to have been Syria, where, in their late phase, the floor mosaics of Antioch exhibit similar transformations of the classical style under the impact of a local tradition. This would be consistent with the iconographical observation of other scholars that the typical Syrian humped ox occurs in some Genesis scenes, and with the idea that the pictures of the Rossano Gospels reflect a liturgical order familiar in Antioch.

Yet this does not necessarily mean that all three purple codices were made in Antioch. Another center within the Syrian orbit must also be taken into consideration: that is Jerusalem, which, after the Council of Chalcedon in 451, became the fifth patriarchate. A connection to Jerusalem is suggested by the Pilate miniatures of the Rossano Gospels (Plates 30–31), and those of the Communion of the Apostles (Figures XV–XVI), which, if we are not mistaken, are copies of monumental compositions of some *loca sancta* in Jerusalem.

Apparently some miniatures of the Rabbula Gospels from 586 A.D. also reflect monumental compositions in Jerusalem (Plates 36–38), although we know for sure that this manuscript was made in Zagba in Mesopotamia. The figure style of this Syriac Gospels has the same characteristics as those we noticed in the miniatures of the three purple manuscripts, and this indicates that, at least in the sixth century, the Syrian style did not differ essentially in Greek and Syriac manuscripts. Even the pictures of the seventh-century Syriac Bible (Plates 39–40, Figures XII–XIII), still reflect a strong Hellenistic heritage within a specific Syrian tradition. One is justified in speaking of Syro-Palestinian art as that of a stylistically homogeneous area.

Returning to the Latin West and to Rome, where we began, there is good reason to believe that the Corpus Christi College Gospels (Plates 41–42), was made either in Rome or elsewhere in Italy at the end of the sixth century, and there is no reason to doubt the tradition that it was sent as a gift by Pope Gregory to Saint Augustine, the first Archbishop of Canterbury. What is most striking is the difference between these Gospels and the Greek and Syriac manuscripts of the same century. The painterly style of the classical tradition, so much better preserved in the East despite its succumbing to hinterland influences, has given way in the West to a linear style which not only flattens the figure, but begins to develop a rhythmic quality in the linear design which must be seen as the beginning of a process of intentional abstraction.

One thing is clear: in the provinces the transformation of the classical style into a more abstract mode proceeded at a faster pace than in those parts of Italy which remained under the influence of Rome. This is quite obvious from the miniatures of the *Vergilius Romanus* of the end of the fifth century (Plates 11–14), where this transformation has gone further than in the undoubtedly later Saint Augustine Gospels. Yet the localization of this Vergil manuscript is still an open question. A recent attempt to attribute the miniatures to an Eastern artist, in our opinion, carries no conviction. True, in Eastern art also, especially in floor mosaics, there occurs a far-reaching simplification in the design of the human figure but, at least in works of respectable quality, the loss of the organic structure of the body does not go as far as in the Vergil miniatures (Plate 13), where the design is subordinated to an abstract linear rhythm, with a strong ornamental organization typical of Western art in those regions where a "barbaric" style began to assert itself. The face shown in strong, exaggerated profile is another element very rare in the East but more frequent in Western art. This feature is, for example, very strongly marked in the ivory plaques from Kranenburg in the Metropolitan Museum of Art in New York which have been ascribed to fifth-century Gaul. Although this does not prove that the Vergil manuscript originated in Gaul, it is nevertheless one of the provinces that, in any future discussion of the localization of the Vergil manuscript, should be taken into consideration.

Another unsolved problem is the localization of the seventh-century Ashburnham Pentateuch (Plates 44–47). The highly developed sense for dramatic action, the exotic dress, the exuberance of the fantastic architectural settings, the sensitivity to a rich decorative color scheme, all speak in favor of a very important center of book production. Yet no other miniatures are known which relate to those of the Pentateuch either stylistically or iconographically. Its Genesis cycle is quite independent of any Eastern cycle such as that of the Cotton or Vienna Genesis, or to the Roman cycles, such as the mosaics of Santa Maria Maggiore or the frescoes in Old Saint Peter's. However it has been noticed that the influence of the Ashburn-

XVII

ham Pentateuch can be felt in later Spanish book illumination, and this seems to narrow somewhat the problem of whether the Pentateuch might have been produced in Spain or come from a region which had exerted a strong influence on Spain, most likely North Africa. No doubt Carthage was a leading and influential Early Christian center, particularly when Saint Augustine was bishop in nearby Hippo. There are in the museum at Carthage two battered marble reliefs showing the Nativity of Christ and the Adoration of the Magi, whose figures display an agitated drapery style not unlike that of some figures in the Ashburnham Pentateuch. Surely this is not enough evidence to ascribe the Ashburnham Pentateuch to Carthage, and yet such a lead should be pursued.

With the Codex Amiatinus in Florence, a Bible which was produced at Jarrow-Wearmouth in Northumbria around 700 A.D. and copied there from Cassiodorus' *Codex Grandior*, executed at Vivarium in Calabria, we have reached the point where the Early Christian tradition clashes with the emerging Middle Ages. The title miniature, with Ezra rewriting the various books of the Old Testament (Plate 48), is the faithful copy of an early Byzantine evangelist portrait, while with the Maiestas picture before the New Testament (Figure XVII), a new tradition begins in which the composition no longer adheres to the concept of natural space. A new and abstract compositional principle has been devised according to which Christ, instead of hovering in the clouds, has become the center of an ornamental geometric pattern. Yet it is an unsettled question whether the two miniatures were executed by a migrant Italian or a native Anglo-Saxon artist.

From this point on, the history of book illumination would no longer deal with accidental and sporadic remains, but with an increasing amount of material whose places of origin can be narrowed down to closer regional limits and a specific monastery often determined. At the same time, book illumination had lost the ecumenical character which distinguished the products of the Late Antique and Early Christian periods.

Selected Bibliography

GENERAL BIBLIOGRAPHY

E. Bethe. *Buch und Bild im Altertum*, ed. E. Kirsten. Leipzig 1945.

T. Birt. *Die Buchrolle in der Kunst*. Leipzig 1907.

A. M. Friend, Jr. "The Portraits of the Evangelists in Greek and Latin Manuscripts," *Art Studies* 1927, 115ff. and 1929, 3ff.

S. J. Gasiorowski. *Malarstwo Minjaturowe Grecko-Rzymskie*. Krakow 1928.

H. Gerstinger. *Die griechische Buchmalerei*. Vienna 1926.

K. Weitzmann. *Ancient Book Illumination*. Cambridge (Mass.) 1959.

————. *Illustrations in Roll and Codex. A Study of the Origin and Method of Text Illustration*. 2nd ed. Princeton 1970.

————. *Studies in Classical and Byzantine Manuscript Illumination*, ed. H. L. Kessler. Chicago 1971.

BIBLIOGRAPHY TO INDIVIDUAL MANUSCRIPTS

Plates 1–4

Fragmenta et Picturae Vergiliana Codicis Vaticani Latini 3225 (Codices e Vaticanis selecti, vol. I). 2nd ed. (facsimile). Rome 1930.

J. de Wit. *Die Miniaturen des Vergilius Vaticanus*. Amsterdam 1959.

Plate 5

H. Degering and A. Boeckler. *Die Quedlinburger Italafragmente* (facsimile). Berlin 1932.

Plate 6

S. J. Gasiorowski. "A Fragment of a Greek Illustrated Papyrus from Antinoë," *Journal of Egyptian Archaeology* XVII (1931), 1ff.

E. G. Turner. "The Charioteers from Antinoë," *Journal of Hellenic Studies* XCIII (1973), 192ff.

Plates 7–10

A. Calderini, A. M. Ceriani, A. Mai. *Ilias Ambrosiana* (Fontes Ambrosiani XXVIII) (facsimile). Bern and Olten 1943.

R. Bianchi Bandinelli. *Hellenistic Byzantine Miniatures of the Iliad*. Olten 1955.

Plates 11–14

Picturae Ornamenta Complura Scripturae Specimina Codicis Vaticani 3867 (Codices e Vaticanis selecti, vol. II) (facsimile). Rome 1902.

E. Rosenthal. *The Illuminations of the Vergilius Romanus*. Zürich 1972.

Plates 15–20

A. von Premerstein, K. Wessely, J. Mantuani. Dioscurides, *Codex Aniciae Julianae picturis illustratus* (Codices Graeci et Latini photogr. depicti, vol. X) (facsimile). Leiden 1906.

P. Buberl. *Die Byzantinischen Handschriften*, vol. I (Beschreibendes Verzeichnis der illuminierten Handschriften in Österreich, vol. VIII, pt. 4). Leipzig 1937, 1ff.

H. Gerstinger. *Dioscurides, Codex Vindobonensis med. gr. 1* (facsimile). Graz 1970.

Plates 21–22

J. J. Tikkanen. "Die Genesismosaiken von S. Marco in Venedig und ihr Verhältnis zu den Miniaturen der Cottonbibel," *Acta Societatis Scientiarum Fennicae* **XVII**. Helsinki 1889, 99ff.

K. Weitzmann, "Observations on the Cotton Genesis Fragments," *Late Classical and Mediaeval Studies in Honor of A. M. Friend, Jr.* Princeton 1955, 112ff.

Plates 23–28

W. von Hartel and F. Wickhoff, *Die Wiener Genesis* (facsimile). Vienna 1895.

H. Gerstinger. *Die Wiener Genesis* (facsimile). Vienna 1931.

P. Buberl. *Die Byzantinischen Handschriften,* vol. I (Beschreibendes Verzeichnis der illuminierten Handschriften in Österreich, vol. VIII, pt. 4). Leipzig 1937, 65ff.

Plates 29–33

A. Muñoz. *Il Codice Purpureo di Rossano* (facsimile). Rome 1907.

W. C. Loerke. "The Miniatures of the Trial in the Rossano Gospels," *Art Bulletin* **XLIII** (1961), 171ff.

Plates 34–38

C. Cecchelli, G. Furlani, M. Salmi. *The Rabbula Gospels* (facsimile). Olten and Lausanne 1959.

J. Leroy. *Les Manuscrits Syriaques à Peintures.* Paris 1964, 139ff.

K. Weitzmann. "Loca Sancta and the Representational Arts of Palestine," *Dumbarton Oaks Papers* **XXVIII** (1974), 31ff.

Plates 39–40

H. Omont. "Peintures de l'Ancien Testament dans un manuscrit syriaque du VIIe au VIIIe siècle," *Monuments Piot* **XVII** (1909), 85ff.

J. Leroy, *op. cit.*, 208ff.

Plates 41–42

F. Wormald. *The Miniatures in the Gospels of St. Augustine* (facsimile). Cambridge 1954.

Plate 43

H. Shaw and F. Madden. *Illuminated Ornaments selected from Manuscripts and Early Printed Books.* London 1833, pls. I–IV.

C. Nordenfalk. *Die spätantiken Kanontafeln.* Göteborg, 1938, 127ff.

————. "The Apostolic Canontables," *Essais en l'honneur de Jean Porcher,* ed. O. Pächt. Paris 1963, 17ff.

Plates 44–47

O. von Gebhard. *The Miniatures of the Ashburnham Pentateuch* (facsimile). London 1883.

B. Narkiss. "Towards a Further Study of the Ashburnham Pentateuch," *Cahiers Archéologiques* **XIX** (1969), 45ff.

J. Gutmann. "The Jewish Origin of the Ashburnham Pentateuch Miniatures," *Jewish Quarterly Review* **XLIV** (1953), 55ff.

Plate 48

R. L. S. Bruce-Mitford. "The Cassiodorus-Ezra Miniature in the Codex Amiatinus," in T. D. Kendrick et al. *Codex Lindisfarnensis.* Olten and Lausanne 1960, 143ff.

P. J. Nordhagen. "An Italo-Byzantine Painter at the Scriptorium of Coelfrith," *Studia Romana in honorem Petri Krarup.* Odense 1976, 138ff.

Figure I

K. Weitzmann, *Ancient Book Illumination,* Cambridge, Mass., 1959, 100ff. and Plate LI, 107.

Figure II

K. Weitzmann, *The Oxyrhynchus Papyri* XXII, 1954, pp. 85ff. and Plate **XI**.

Figures IV–VI

J. Strzygowski, "Die Calenderbilder des Chronographen vom Jahre 354," *Jahrbuch des Archäologischen Instituts,* I. Ergänzungsheft, Berlin, 1888.

C. Nordenfalk, "Der Kalender vom Jahre 354 und die lateinische Buchmalerei des IV. Jahrhunderts," *Göteborgs Kungl. Vetenskaps och Vitterhets-Samhälles Handlinger,* Ser. A.5,2, 1936, 28ff.

H. Stern, *Le Calendrier de 354. Étude de son texte et ses illustrations,* Paris, 1953.

Figures VIII–X

G. Jachmann, Terentius. *Codex Vaticanus Latinus 3868* (facsimile).

Codices e Vaticanis Selecti, vol. XVIII, Leipzig, 1929.

L. W. Jones and C. R. Morey, *The Miniatures of the Manuscripts of Terence,* 2 vols., Princeton, 1931.

Figure XI

H. Omont, "Fragments du Manuscrit de la Genèse de R. Cotton, conservés parmi les papiers de Peiresc," *Mémoires de la Société des Antiquaires de France,* LIII (1895), 163ff.

————. *Miniatures des plus anciens manuscrits grecs de la Bibliothèque Nationale du VIe an XIVe siècle,* 2nd ed., Paris, 1929, pp. 10f. and Plate.

Figure XIV

H. Omont, *Miniatures,* pp. 1ff. and Plates A–B.

A. Grabar, *Les Peintures de l'Evangéliaire de Sinope,* Paris, 1948.

Descriptions of Manuscripts

LIST OF COLOR PLATES AND BLACK-AND-WHITE FIGURES

I. Vergilius Vaticanus

Vatican Library, cod. lat. 3225
76 fols. 219 × 196 mm
In the Renaissance the manuscript belonged to two famous collectors, Pietro Bembo and then Fulvio Orsini, who bequeathed it to the Vatican Library in 1600.
Plate 1. *Georgics* fol. 4v
Plate 2. *Sack of Troy* fol. 19r
Plate 3. *Death of Dido* fol. 40r
Plate 4. *Trojan Council* fol. 73v

II. Quedlinburg Itala

Deutsche Staatsbibliothek, Berlin/ DDR, Cod. theol. lat. fol. 485
1 + 5 fols. approx. 305 × 205 mm
The six leaves from the Book of Kings, used in 1618 as binding material by Asmus Reitel of Quedlinburg, were discovered in 1865 and given in 1875/76 to the Royal Library.
Plate 5. *Saul and Samuel* fol. 2r

III. The Charioteer Papyrus

London, The Egypt Exploration Society

fragment 120 × 75 mm
Found in 1914 by Johnson in Antinoë in a rubbish mound.
Plate 6. *Charioteers*

IV. Ilias Ambrosiana
Milan, Ambrosian Library, Cod. F. 205 Inf.
The manuscript was in Constantinople in the later Middle Ages when the tituli in the miniatures were added. In 1608 Cardinal Federico Borromeo acquired it at Naples for the Ambrosian Library.
Plate 7. *Iliad* pict. XXXIV
Plate 8. *Iliad* pict. XLVII
Plate 9. *Iliad* pict. XX–XXI
Plate 10. *Iliad* pict. XXXVII

V. Vergilius Romanus
Vatican Library, cod. lat. 3867
309 fols. 332 × 323 mm
The manuscript was at Saint Denis until the fifteenth century. When it came to the Vatican is not quite clear.
Plate 11. *Eclogues* fol. 1r
Plate 12. *Georgics* fol. 44v
Plate 13. *Aeneas & Dido: Convivium* fol. 100v
Plate 14. *Aeneas & Dido in Cave* fol. 106r
Figure III. *Vergil* fol. 3v

VI. Vienna Dioscurides
Vienna, Nationalbibliothek, cod. med. gr. 1
491 fols. 380 × 330 mm
In the fourteenth century it was used by the monk Neophytus of the monastery of the Prodromus of Petra, Constantinople. In 1569 it was sold, through the offices of Augerius de Busbecke, to Emperor Maximilian II by the son of Hamon, physician to Sultan Suleiman II.
Plate 15. *Anicia Juliana* fol. 6v
Plate 16. *Seven Physicians* fol. 3v

Plate 17. *Dioscurides* fol. 5v
Plate 18. *Violet* fol. 148v
Plate 19. *Coral* fol. 391v
Plate 20. *Birds* fol. 483v
Figure VII. *Serpents* fol. 411r

VII. Cotton Genesis
London, The British Library, cod. Cotton Otho B. VI
294 fols. 273 × 222 mm (approx.)
The manuscript was a gift from two bishops of Philippi to King Henry VIII. In the seventeenth century it was in the possession of Sir Robert Cotton, who lent it to Peiresc (in 1618), who intended to make a facsimile with engravings (Figure XI). It burned in 1731 in the Ashburnham House, then the British Museum, and only about 150 charred fragments remain.
Plate 21. *Abraham & Angels* fol. 26v
Plate 22. *Lot's House* Bristol IVv

VIII. Vienna Genesis
Vienna, Nationalbibliothek, cod. theol. gr. 31
279 fols. 335 × 250 mm
In the fourteenth century the manuscript was in Venice and entered the Imperial Library in 1664.
Plate 23. *Deluge* pict. 3
Plate 24. *Rebecca & Eliezer* pict. 13
Plate 25. *Joseph's Departure* pict. 30
Plate 26. *Temptation of Joseph* pict. 31
Plate 27. *Joseph in Prison* pict. 33
Plate 28. *Blessing of Ephraim & Manasseh* pict. 45

IX. Rossano Gospels
Rossano (Calabria), Il Duomo di Rossano
188 fols. 307 × 260 mm
An old treasure of the Cathedral of Rossano, it was first mentioned by

Cesare Malpica, a Neapolitan journalist, in 1845.

Plate 29. *Raising of Lazarus* fol. 1r

Plate 30. *Christ Before Pilate* fol. 8r

Plate 31. *Christ Before Pilate* fol. 8v

Plate 32. *Good Samaritan* fol. 7v

Plate 33. *St. Mark* fol. 121r

Figure XV. *Communion of Apostles* fol. 3v

Figure XVI. *Communion of Apostles* fol. 4r

Frontispiece *Title to Canons* fol. 5r

X. Rabbula Gospels

Florence, Laurentian Library, cod. Plut. I, 56

292 fols. 336 × 266 mm

Written in 586 A.D. at the monastery of St. John of Zagba, Mesopotamia. In the eleventh century in the monastery of S. Maria of Maiphuc, then in the monastery of Kanubin, and in 1497 it entered the Laurenziana.

Plate 34. *Canon Table* fol. 4v

Plate 35. *Matthew & John* fol. 9v

Plate 36. *Ascension* fol. 13v

Plate 37. *Christ Enthroned* fol. 14r

Plate 38. *Pentecost* fol. 14v

XI. The Syriac Bible of Paris

Paris, Bibliothèque Nationale, cod. syr. 341

246 fols. 312 × 230 mm

Presumably from the Episcopal Library of Sjirt (near Lake Van), a place where it may have been produced. Entered the Bibliothèque Nationale in 1909.

Plate 39. *Job* fol. 46r

Plate 40. *Moses Before Pharaoh* fol. 8r

Figure XII. *Sirach* fol. 218v

Figure XIII. *Joshua* fol. 52v

XII. The Gospels of St. Augustine

Cambridge, Corpus Christi College,

cod. 286

265 + V fols. 250 × 190 mm

Formerly owned by St. Augustine's, Canterbury, and presented by Matthew Parker, Archbishop of Canterbury, to Corpus Christi College in 1575.

Plate 41. *New Testament Scenes* fol. 125r

Plate 42. *St. Luke* fol. 129v

XIII. The London Canon Tables

London, The British Library, cod. add. 5111

2 fols. 220 × 158 mm

Bound into a Greek Gospel Book dated 1189 A.D. which is said to have come from Mount Athos.

Plate 43. *Canon Table* fol. 11r

XIV. Ashburnham Pentateuch

Paris, Bibliothèque Nationale, cod. n. acq. lat. 2334

142 fols. 371 × 321 mm

The manuscript was at Tours from the ninth century until 1843 when it was stolen from the Cathedral Library and sold to the Duke of Ashburnham in 1847. Entered the Bibliothèque Nationale in 1888.

Plate 44. *Cain & Abel* fol. 6r

Plate 45. *Deluge* fol. 9r

Plate 46. *Isaac & Rebecca* fol. 21r

Plate 47. *Moses Receiving Law* fol. 76r

XV. Codex Amiatinus

Florence, Laurentian Library, cod. Amiat. 1

1029 fols. 500 × 340 mm

Since the end of the ninth or beginning of the tenth century in the Abbey of San Salvatore di Monte Amiato (near Siena). In 1786 in the Castello Nuovo at Florence.

Plate 48. *Ezra* fol. Vr

Figure XVII. *Christ in Majesty* fol. 786v

ADDITIONAL BLACK AND WHITE FIGURES

Figure I

Paris, Bibliothèque Nationale, cod. suppl. gr. 1294
340 × 115 mm
Acquired 1900.
Romance Papyrus

Figure II

London, The Egypt Exploration Society
235 × 106 mm
Found at Oxyrhynchos (Pap. 2331).
Heracles Papyrus

Figure IV

Vatican Library, cod. Barb. lat. 2154
55 fols. 276 × 206 mm
The seventeenth-century drawings are based on an intermediary Carolingian copy of the original Calendar of Filocalus written in 354 A.D. in Rome for a Christian by the name of Valentinus.
Constans II fol. 13r

Figure V

Roma fol. 2r

Figure VI

Month of March fol. 18r

Figure VIII

Vatican Library, cod. lat. 3868
92 fols. 343 × 293 mm
The manuscript was written by the monk Hrodgarius and painted by Adelricus in the third decennium of the ninth century in Lorraine, according to the most recent investigation. Already listed in the catalogue of the Vatican Library by Bartholomaeus Platina in 1475 under Sixtus IV. (W. Koehler and F. Mütherich, *Die Hofschule Kaiser Lothars* [Die Karolingischen Miniaturen, Bd. IV], Berlin 1971, pp. 85ff. and pls. 28–61).
Terence fol. 2r

Figure X

Scene from Adelphoe fol. 60v

Figure XI

Paris, Bibliothèque Nationale, cod. franç. 9530
325 fols. 250 × 380 mm
One of the two watercolors by Daniel Rabel made in 1622 for Nicholas-Claude Fabri de Peiresc for a planned facsimile edition of the Cotton Genesis.
Genesis fol. 32r

Figure XIV

Paris, Bibliothèque Nationale, cod. suppl. gr. 1286
43 fols. 200 × 180 mm
Acquired in 1900 from a French officer, Jean de la Taille, who had bought it the year before at Sinope (Black Sea).
Fig Tree fol. 30v

Color Plates
and Commentaries

PLATE 1

VERGILIUS VATICANUS
fol. 5v *Georgics*

In his didactic poem, the *Georgics*, Vergil tells the story of two jealous bulls fighting over a beautiful cow in Sila in the Apennines (III, 209ff.). Against a sky that turns from pink to light blue, two enraged bulls charge each other, about to lock horns in front of a tree with a gold-striated trunk and feathery leaves. The beautiful white cow, in a haughty attitude, looks on, while the defeated bull, whose color is changed from brown to white to balance that of the cow, is repeated at the right, charging a tree trunk—an exercise to build new strength for the resumption of the fight.

Vergil did not invent this story, a familiar tale which occurs in several ancient writers including Pseudo-Oppian, Aelian, and Pliny. In an eleventh-century Pseudo-Oppian manuscript in Venice, this episode (*Cynegetica* II, 43ff.) is illustrated in no fewer than four consecutive frameless scenes in the fashion of papyrus illustration (Figures I–II), faithfully reflecting a second-third century archetype. Here, the scene of the fighting bulls is so similar to that of the Vatican Vergil that a common, and surely a Greek, archetype must be assumed. The illustrator of the Vatican codex, who worked in Rome in the early fifth century, has reduced the narrative cycle to two scenes, creating for them a unifying landscape influenced by fresco painting, and framing the miniature to give a panel-like appearance.

SED NON NULLA MAGIS VIRES INDUSTRIA FIRMAT.

1

PLATE 2

VERGILIUS VATICANUS
fol. 19r *Sack of Troy*

In Books II and III of the *Aeneid*, Vergil tells the story of the Sack of Troy in great detail, drawing upon a Greek epic poem of the Trojan cycle recounting among its episodes the well-known story of the Trojan Horse. The miniature depicts the moment when the traitor Sinon opens the trap door of the Wooden Horse and one of the Achaeans, Odysseus, is "sliding down the lowered rope," while other Achaeans are engaged in killing the Trojans who had been feasting, reclining against crescent-shaped bolsters. The scene is enclosed by the wall of Troy. Outside the wall a ship is visible under the moon and stars, indicating that the surprise attack took place at night.

Vergil speaks only of attacking the guards, and the killing of the banqueters is not explained by his text. This and other details indicate that the illustrator had available another source, most probably an illustrated *Iliupersis* of Stesichorus, illustrations of which are preserved on a plaque of *piombino* (pulverized marble) from the first century in the *Museo Capitolino* in Rome. Here we see, in the center, a similar composition of an encompassing city wall and individual combat scenes separated more sharply from each other than in the more unified composition of the Vatican miniature. Most important, in this tablet the opening of the horse by a trap door and the letting down of Odysseus is so similar that a common archetype must be assumed, reaching back at least as far as the first century, the date of the marble plaque, and before the invention of the codex.

ETIAMARGIONEFHALANAINSTRUCTISNAUIB·IBAT
ATENEDOTACITAEFERAMICASILENTIALUNAE
LITORANOTAPETENSFLAMMASQUATRIGIAPUPPIS
EXTULERATFATISQUEDEUMDEFENSUSINIQUIS·
INCLUSUTERODANAOSETPINEAFURTIM

PLATE 3

VERGILIUS VATICANUS
fol. 40r *Death of Dido*

Dido's dramatic death, one of the most important events of the *Aeneid*, is represented by two miniatures, one of the moment just before, and the other immediately after, her suicide (IV, 645ff.). In order to emphasize its significance, the illustrator has made the former scene, in which Dido raises the sword before plunging it into her bare breast, into one of the few full-page miniatures. We see Dido lying on a couch atop a pyre so high that she had to climb up by a ladder, which leans against it. Vergil made it quite clear (V, 494) that the pyre was erected in the inner court under the sky, but the artist has placed the event illogically in the interior of a splendid palace chamber with colored marble incrustation familiar in the fourth century. A high coffered ceiling, drawn perspectively, is seen above a window, and at the left there is an entrance door with a drawn curtain. This very conspicuous door does not take into consideration the foreshortening of the side wall. Here the perspective of the classical past has given way to a more abstract principle, according to which full visibility is more important than correct spatial relationships.

Whereas in the two previous miniatures the illustrator was able to copy more or less literally from earlier Greek book illumination, in this case he adapts a traditional compositional scheme, perhaps of a dying Alcestis from an illustrated Euripides text.

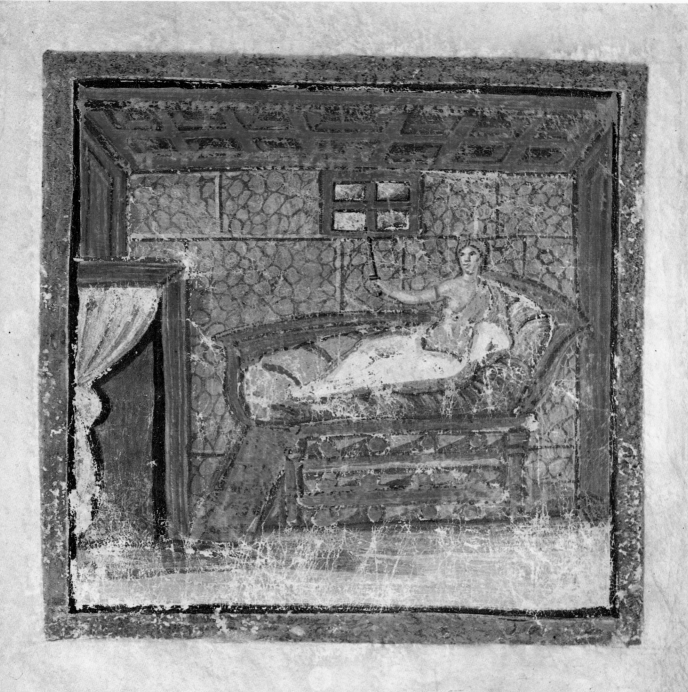

4

PLATE 4

VERGILIUS VATICANUS
fol. 73v *Trojan Council*

When the Trojans were encamped at the mouth of the Tiber they held a meeting at night, over which Ascanius presided, to discuss whom to send to Aeneas. According to Vergil (IX, 176ff.), first Nisus and then Euryalus spoke; in the miniature, however, they are not depicted in lively dispute but appear more like imperial bodyguards, all three dressed in the purple chlamys; they are flanked on either side by groups of soldiers whose cinnabar-colored shields provide a striking color accent. Two men seen from the back stand in the foreground. One is inscribed "Aletes," the third speaker in the assembly, who according to Vergil was "stricken in years," but is depicted as quite youthful. The other is not named and cannot be explained by Vergil's text. He is placed there apparently for reasons of the rigorous symmetry which pervades the whole picture.

In his intention to create a hieratic composition the artist obviously has taken liberties with the text and, instead of a simple strip-like composition, such as one finds in the assembly pictures of the Milan *Iliad*, he seems to be influenced by a monumental composition of some kind of tribunal scene. A city wall, not called for in a camping scene, fills evenly the four spandrels of the oval composition, more abstracted and ornamentalized than in the *Iliupersis* picture (Plate 2).

The illustrator of the *Vergilius Vaticanus*, while making use of an older iconographic tradition when possible, also experiments with new compositional ideas borrowed from other media.

PLATE 5

QUEDLINBURG ITALA
fol. 2r *Saul and Samuel*

In an almost breathtakingly rapid sequence, the episode of Saul's meeting with Samuel after the defeat of the Amalekites is depicted in four scenes covering only verses 13–33 of I. Samuel 15. It staggers the imagination to picture what a fully illustrated manuscript of the two books of Samuel and the two books of Kings must have looked like. The first scene shows Samuel's arrival on a two-horse chariot, while Saul makes a sacrifice, the whole having the air of an imperial Roman ceremony. Then Samuel, angered that Saul has not destroyed all the spoils, runs away with Saul following, clutching the end of the prophet's mantle and rending it. In the next scene, Saul (we believe he is wrongly inscribed Agag) asks forgiveness of his sins and immediately thereafter Samuel and Saul pray together to the Lord. Finally, in front of the walled city of Gilgal, Samuel himself kills Agag, king of the Amalekites, while Saul looks on.

While iconographically the picture is divided into compartments, artistically the illustrator has tried to unify the scenes within each register by adding a pink and light blue sky which rises above a mountain range with sketchy, decorative buildings, a sky not unlike that in the illustration to Vergil's *Georgics* (Plate 1). The figures, as well, show the same elegant style, with occasional gold striations. Both artists may even have worked in the same scriptorium in Rome, in the early fifth century.

PLATE 6

The Charioteer Papyrus

Of the pitifully few fragments remaining of papyrus illustration, the best in design and color depicts a group of charioteers; five figures are easily recognizable, while of a sixth only a small segment is left. They are identifiable by their dress: each wears an armored vest laced up the front to protect him in falls, a belt and a crash helmet; one holds a whip. They seem to emerge from a building, suggested by a simple yellow arch. Three are dressed in green, one in blue, and one in red, representing the factions of the Roman circus. The fourth such faction, the white, is not represented in the picture.

This fragment is all that remains of a codex page from about the second half of the fifth century, with a few lines written in large capitals indicating that we are dealing with a manuscript which must have been very sumptuous, and of stately size. But the few letters on both sides of the page are unfortunately insufficient to identify the text, and while it may be tempting to think of Book XXIII of the *Iliad* where races took place at the funeral games of Achilles, we cannot even be sure whether the text is from an epic poem or prose.

The figure style of the fragment, found in 1914 at Antinoë, with its tendency to flatten out the body by straight heavy outlines, with round faces, and low foreheads, is typically Egyptian and is related to that of the Milan *Iliad* (Plate 8), and even more so to that of the Cotton Genesis (Plates 21–22).

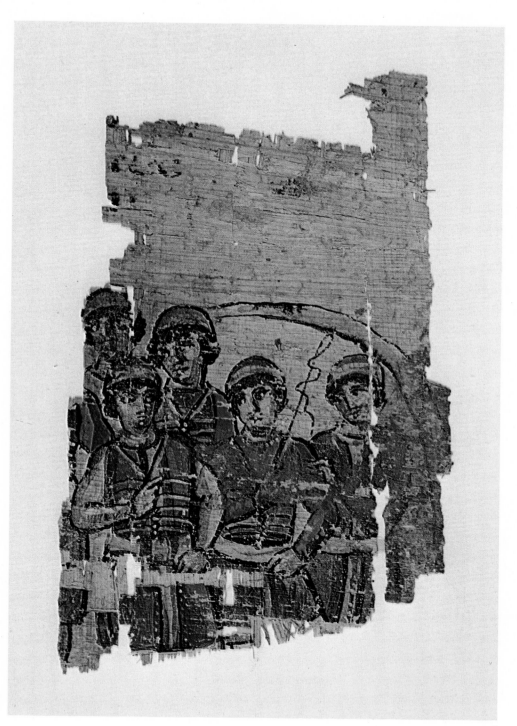

PLATE 7

ILIAS AMBROSIANA
pict. XXXIV *Capture of Dolon*

The story of Book X, in which Dolon, the Trojan spy, falls into the hands of the Achaeans, is told in two consecutive scenes, placed side by side in true narrative fashion so that the eye quickly moves from one to the other. Dolon has disguised himself in an olive-colored wolf-skin and is caught by the neck by Odysseus, who is dressed in a tunic and an orange-colored mantle, whose end billows out in the wind, increasing the dramatic effect of the very agitated group. Diomedes, dressed in full armour and rendered in a swaying pose, looks on. In the next scene Diomedes is drawing his sword in order to kill Dolon, but, in contradiction to the text of the *Iliad*, it is Odysseus who decapitates him after having gruesomely dismembered him. The illustrator has taken other liberties with the text and given Odysseus the usual *pilos*, the pointed cap by which he is always recognized, and Diomedes a crested helmet, although both should wear caps of hide. Here too the wide stride and vivid action of the two heroes add to the turbulent effect of the scene. The hovering bust of Night is contradicted by the conventional impressionistic colors of the sky, changing from pinkish violet to light blue, whereby the scene is, for obvious reasons of visibility, placed at either dawn or sunset.

The *Iliad* miniatures, to be dated toward the end of the fifth century, have preserved much of the Hellenistic tradition, and the Dolon miniature belongs to that group of fragments which best preserves the style of the papyrus roll illustration.

PLATE 8

ILIAS AMBROSIANA
pict. XLVII *Achilles*

Achilles, barefooted, stands in front of his rose-colored tent and offers a libation upon a flaming altar, holding the lustral bowl in his right hand and leaning on a spear with the left (XVI, 220ff.). He wears a purple cloak which exposes part of his body and fittingly covers his head. He is praying to Zeus, who is depicted as an *imago clipeata* (a bust in a shield) above some trees, to protect Patroclus, who with his weapons has gone into battle against Hector.

In this miniature the illustrator has outgrown the figure scale of all the other miniatures and depicted Achilles in a monumental fashion; it is quite significant that he should have done so in this one case for the leading hero of the *Iliad*. This suggests the influence of monumental painting and yet does not imply that a fresco of this subject was actually copied. In the enlarged picture area allowed him in a codex page, the illustrator was quite capable of enlarging a smaller figure from the papyrus roll tradition.

Despite this monumental effect, the body of Achilles lacks corporeality, because the traditional firm stance has been abandoned in favour of a swaying pose, and the outlines of the figure have been straightened and the body thereby flattened. In this we see a deviation from the classical norm and a similar reappearance of older Egyptian features, as in the Cotton Genesis miniatures (Plates 21–22).

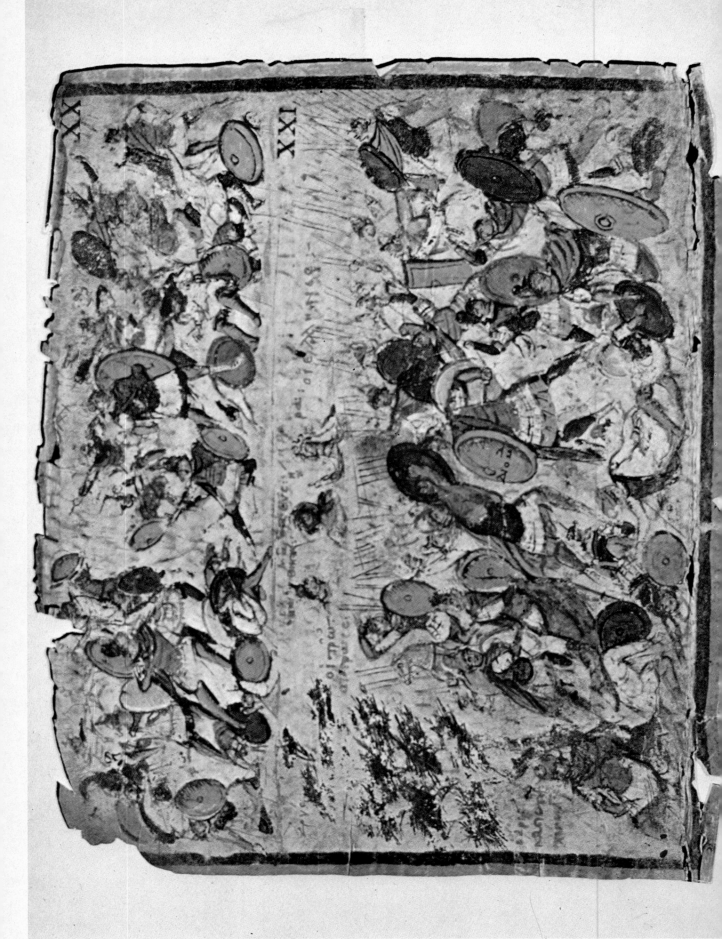

PLATE 9

ILIAS AMBROSIANA
pict. XX–XXI *Battle Scene*

To a special group of miniatures within this manuscript belong the very crowded battle scenes of which, in this picture, we see two. The text on the back contains verses 634–57 of Book V, but in the first scene there is no single feature which can be explained by these or the following verses. The two over-life-size combatants in the center of the second scene are most probably the Trojan Sarpedon and the Achaean Tlepolemus (inscribed by a later hand wrongly as Diomedes) who, according to the text, hurl spears against each other, while in the miniature the latter attacks with a sword. This interpretation is supported by the fact that in the lower left the wounded Sarpedon—the only surely identifiable figure—is depicted seated under a tree. The general lack of agreement with the text can most easily be explained by assuming that the illustrator copied huge complex wall paintings, adjusting them only superficially to the events described in the Homeric poem. The only elements of an older *Iliad* tradition are most likely the single combat scene in the center, which appears somewhat isolated from the rest of the raging battle, and the wounded Sarpedon. This would indicate that the miniature of the archetype had two concise scenes side by side, just as the miniature with the Dolon adventure (Plate 7). Whether the onlooking gods Athena, Zeus, and Hera, whose busts hover over a cloudbank, were part of the original composition is undeterminable.

The crowded battlefield with many overlapping figures reminds one of some third-century battle sarcophagi, and the fresco model behind the miniature probably belongs to this period.

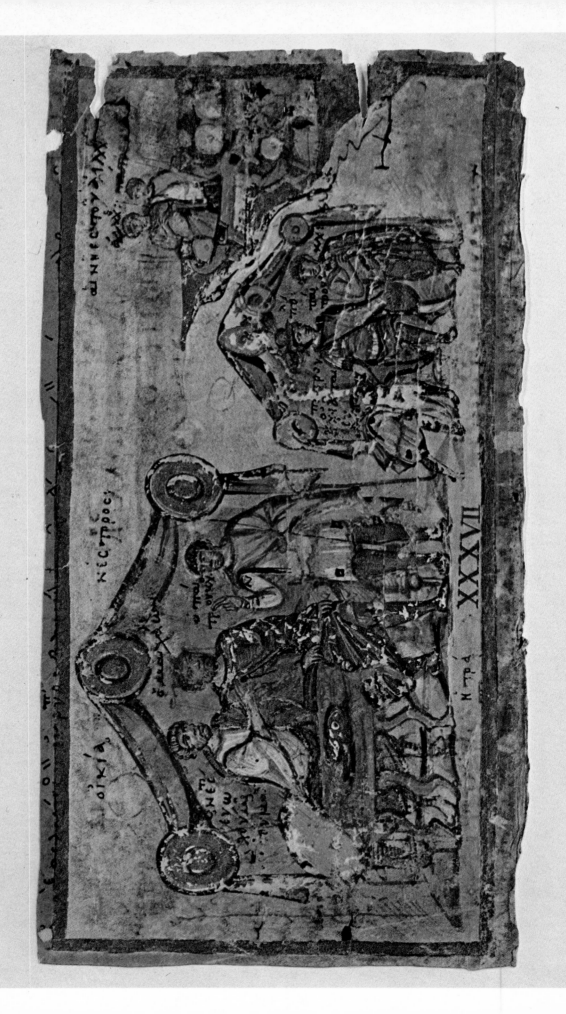

PLATE 10

ILIAS AMBROSIANA
pict **XXXVII** *Nestor and Patroclus*

Three scenes from Book XI are squeezed into the picture frame not in logical sequence but as they best fit into the limited space. At the upper right we see "Achilles . . . standing by the stern of his ship, huge of hull, gazing upon the utter toil of battle" (599ff.). Next follows the scene at the left where the artist has enlarged the figure scale to mark it as what he must have felt was the most important. Here Patroclus, who has refused to be seated, addresses Nestor who sits in his tent behind a table with Machaon (648ff.). The white tunics of the two protagonists and the orange of Patroclus' mantle and the cushion are skillfully used color accents. To the right is a similarly composed tent scene, dwarfed in scale, in which Patroclus attends to the wounded Eurypylus who has been hit in the thigh by an arrow (842ff.). The third figure, who looks like Achilles, is not called for by the text, which, as a whole, is followed very closely in this miniature.

While the system of illustration, as in the Dolon adventure (Plate 7), reflects that of the papyrus rolls into whose writing columns each of the three scenes could easily be fitted, in style this is the most advanced. Whereas the three previously discussed miniatures, in spite of their dependence on different kinds of models, show a homogeneity in their figure treatment, with vivid actions often exaggerated, the artist of our miniature prefers immovable, frontal figures which foreshadow features on which the mediaeval style will be based.

PLATE 11

VERGILIUS ROMANUS
fol. 1r *Eclogues*

Whereas the illustrations of the *Vergilius Vaticanus* (Plates 1–4) and the Milan *Iliad* (Plates 7–10) are still deeply steeped in a painterly classical tradition, those of the *Vergilius Romanus* show the beginnings of a process of linear abstraction in the design of the human body and the abandonment of natural spatial relationships.

The very first miniature, heading the First Eclogue, still shows remnants of a classical style: Tityrus the cowherd sits at the left under a wide-branched tree and contentedly plays his flute, while three cows peep out from behind the tree; Meliboeus the goatherd, in agreement with the text, leads one of the goats by its horns. Other goats peep out from behind a tree at the right, showing the artist's almost desperate attempt to save the appearance of a spatial setting. At the same time, the unique lack of a frame still shows adherence to the tradition of papyrus illustration.

On the one hand, this is a pretentious manuscript written in an artificial uncial twice the normal size, and on the other, it is illustrated by artists who try to balance weakness in the design of the human body by an unusually large scale, giving to the miniatures a monumentality which is somewhat in contrast to the intimacy of the subject.

The artist who begins the illustration maintains some adherence to natural human proportions and freedom of motion and gesture. With the second miniature, another artist, of a very different background and training, takes over.

TITYRE·TU·PATULE·RECUBANS·SUB·TEGMINE·FAG
SILVESTRE·M·TENVI·MVSAM·MEDITARIS·AVENA
NOS·PATRIAE·FINES·ET·DVLCIA·LINQVIMVS·ARVA
NOS·PATRIAM·FVGIMVS·TV·TITYRE·LENTVS·IN·VMBRA
FORMOSAM·RESONARE·DOCES·AMARYLLIDA·SILVAS
O·MELIBOEE·DEVS·NOBIS·HAEC·OTIA·FECIT
NAMQVE·ERIT·ILLE·MIHI·SEMPER·DEVS·ILLIVS·ARAM
SAEPE·TENER·NOSTRIS·AB·OVILIBVS·IMBVET·AGNVS
ILLE·MEAS·ERRARE·BOVES·VT·CERNIS·ET·IPSVM

12

PLATE 12

VERGILIUS ROMANUS
fol. 44v   *Georgics*

Beginning with the second miniature to the *Eclogues* and consistent throughout
the *Georgics* and the *Aeneid*, we find a style that is quite unlike that of the first
miniature. In a full-page illustration to the third book of the *Georgics* there are
two shepherds, one seated and playing the flute and the other leaning on his
staff and listening. They are stock types of the bucolic repertory, found on
numerous sarcophagi and elsewhere and not particularly related to the passage
from the *Georgics* to which this and a second such miniature on the opposite
page are attached.

There is no groundline: the figures and the animals are suspended and evenly
distributed over the surface, whose yellowish color lacks any association with
nature. Overlappings are carefully avoided and a hut, a few bushes and flowers
equidistant from each other form a tapestry-like pattern. Such a distribution of
elements is very common in Late Antique floor mosaics, and it seems quite
likely that these were the inspiration for the miniature painter who was striving
for an effect of monumentality and patternized surface.

Compared with the shepherds of the preceding miniature, the body structure
is weakened. The garments are treated in a more linear and abstract manner,
emphasizing a rhythm of curving, parallel foldlines. The three-quarter view of
the faces has been replaced by a somewhat stylized profile. Moving away from
the classical tradition, the expressive linear design reflects the mentality of an
artist who is more concerned with decorative qualities than with verisimilitude.

13

PLATE 13

VERGILIUS ROMANUS
fol. 100v   *Aeneas & Dido Convivium*

In order to hear more about the Sack of Ilium from Aeneas, the love-stricken Dido has arranged a banquet (IV, 77ff.). In contrast to the text, which is charged with the emotions of unhappy Dido, the miniature depicts the banqueters in stiff, ceremonial poses. Dido, crowned and bejewelled, is in the exact center, with Aeneas at the left, and another Trojan, characterized like Aeneas by the Phrygian cap, is not accounted for by the text and is apparently added (like the figure matching Aletes in Plate 4) for reasons of symmetry at the right. The artist seems to have limited experience in the design of the human body: he is utterly unable to cope with the problem of the contorted pose of the reclining figure at the right, but what he lacks in understanding of the structure of the human body he compensates for with the lively, swinging rhythms of the garments. He is not an unskilled artist, but he is more concerned with patternization. One will notice that the interior of the palace chamber (in contrast to Plate 3) is compartmentalized by draperies hanging from the frame into three sections, each of which encloses one of the three figures. The three rest on a draped bench with even fold patterns, into which a table is tightly fitted, its top set in the geometric center like a cabochon. The strong symmetry of the composition is enhanced by the two servants serving wine with faces in strict profile. Also abstract are the colors and their separation into three strips, yellow for the floor, purple for the drapery of the couch, and green for the wall. Beginning with the miniature from the *Georgics* (Plate 12) the artist has made steady progress in abstract design.

PLATE 14

VERGILIUS ROMANUS
fol. 108r   *Aeneas & Dido in Cave*

One of the most dramatic episodes in the *Aeneid*, in which Dido and Aeneas
are surprised by a thunderstorm and take refuge in a cave (IV, 160ff.), is
treated in a manner typical of our illustrator: he compartmentalizes the scene,
dividing it into four areas of uneven shape to avoid giving a mechanical
impression. At the lower right Dido and Aeneas, embracing in such a way that
there is no doubt who is the more aggressive, are seated frontally in what looks
more like a box than a cave. To their left are their horses, on a small scale, tied
to a tree and seemingly lifted off the ground with plants as space-fillers beneath
their hooves. Thick raindrops fall from the sky and a soldier in the upper left
protects himself by holding his shield over his head—a realistic feature quite
suggestively rendered. The fourth section is filled by a Trojan soldier in the
conventional pose of a guard, seemingly unaffected by the storm. He sits on top
of the cave, although one would expect him to sit at its entrance. In his avoid-
ance of spatial relationships, the artist demonstrates his intention (as in the
scene from the *Georgics*, Plate 12) to show every feature equidistant from the
beholder.

The expressive quality of the miniature lies in the strong outlining of the
figures and the decorative design of the draperies, which have the quality
achieved in later centuries by woodcuts. Because the manuscript has no relation
to any other, its date has not yet been determined more precisely than the fifth
or sixth century. On paleographical evidence, it has been proposed to narrow it
to the second half of the fifth century.

14

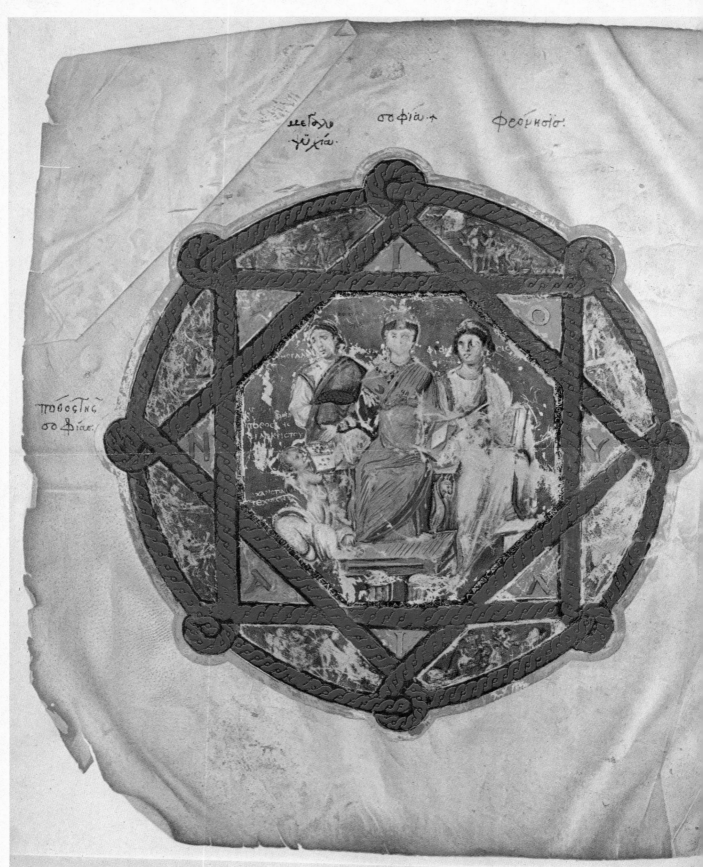

PLATE 15

VIENNA DIOSCURIDES
fol. 6v *Anicia Juliana*

This luxurious herbal contains the oldest dedication miniature in existence, representing the princess Anicia Juliana within an eight-pointed star enclosed by a circle, formed of an intertwined rope. In a stiff ceremonial pose and dressed in a gold-striated *trabea* reflecting the contemporary court style, she sits on a cushioned throne distributing coins and holding the *codicillus*, which distinguishes her as a member of the patriciate. She is flanked by the personifications of Magnanimity, carrying more gold coins in her lap, and Prudence, holding a codex on her raised knee as a symbol of Anicia's learnedness. A third personification, inscribed "Gratitude of the Arts," kneels at the princess's feet. She and a putto holding the dedication copy allude to Anicia as the founder of a church in the suburbs of Constantinople, whose citizens show their gratitude by the gift of this manuscript. The outer spandrels, in grisaille in the Hellenistic manner, show putti working as masons and carpenters, similar to those in the Casa di Vetii in Pompeii, likewise implying Anicia's architectural patronage. The church alluded to in the dedicatory inscription was built in 512–13 A.D., and the manuscript must have been written shortly before this date.

The miniature is an original creation and reflects the most refined style of Constantinople, harmonizing the ceremonial character of the imperial court with the classical tradition as reflected in the personifications, especially the putto holding the book and the putti active in crafts, notwithstanding that the princess was a pious Christian.

16

PLATE 16

VIENNA DIOSCURIDES
fol. 3v *Seven Physicians*

The series of frontispieces begins with two collective pictures, each showing a set of seven famous pharmacologists. The most prominent in the second picture is Galen, who sits in the center as the only one in an easy chair. He is flanked by Crateuas to his right and Dioscurides to his left, both raising hands as a gesture of speech. The pair in the middle zone are Apollonius Mys and Nicander. A paraphrase of the latter's treatise on snake bites is part of the Vienna codex (Figure VII), and he is shown here holding out a plant to a serpent. At the bottom sit Andreas and Rufus, the presumed author of the *carmen de herbis* (Plate 19).

The choice of seven pharmacologists and their being grouped together is clearly inspired by the concept of the Seven Wise Men as they appear on ancient floor mosaics, sitting on a semi-circular bench. Yet compositionally our miniature cannot derive from such models: it is clearly composed of individual, quite self-contained portraits, for whose chairs there was not enough space; thus the figures are rendered sitting on slabs or rocks. For most if not all of them, models must have existed in the form of frontispieces to their treatises. It is significant that the two miniatures with the gathering of the pharmacologists are the earliest we know in which figures are placed before a solid gold ground. There is no reason to doubt that they were executed by the same artist who painted the dedication miniature, who was capable of working in different modes depending on the nature of his models, and who made innovations, like the gold ground, leading the way toward a more abstract concept of space, whereas the individual portraits (e.g., Plate 17) have firmly maintained a classical style.

PLATE 17

V I E N N A   D I O S C U R I D E S
fol. 5v *Dioscurides*

The second of the two author portraits depicts Dioscurides seated in profile and writing in a codex which he holds in his lap. The sensitive head with brown hair and pointed beard corresponds to that in the previous miniature and there may well be the tradition of a life portrait behind it. Before him sits a youthful painter in work clothes on a low bench—thus clearly differentiated as to social status from the scholar. On his easel is fastened with thumbtacks a huge square parchment sheet like that of the actual codex, and on it he paints the mandrake, a root in human shape. He copies it from nature, looking back to a root held in the hands of a personification of Epinoia ("Power of Thought"), clad in a gold-striated chiton and a deep blue shawl, the strongest color accent, over her shoulder and arm. The background, a colonnade with a central niche, is reminiscent of the *scenae frons* of the theatre—an often used formula, not quite in accordance with the concept of a studio, but added apparently for mere decorative splendor.

In the first author portrait as well, where the pharmacist is faced with a very similar personification, inscribed Heuresis ("Invention"), the ill-famed mandrake is depicted above a dog which, according to a legend not recorded by Dioscurides, dies from digging it up.

There was a tradition in Greco-Roman art, in marble reliefs, frescoes, mosaics, and other media, of poets and writers inspired by a muse, and from some such picture our gifted illuminator drew his inspiration.

اي يو پوُر فيروُن

بنفنه

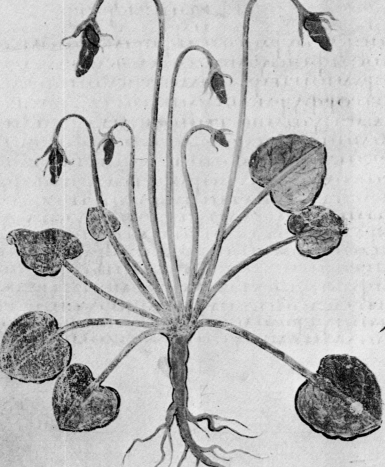

PLATE 18

VIENNA DIOSCURIDES
fol. 148v *Violet*

The few extant fragments of illustrated papyrus herbals show that their normal system of illustration, surviving also in later codices, was the depiction of the plant on top of the writing column with the explanatory text underneath. It is exceptional that in the luxurious Vienna codex, a full page of considerable size (37 x 30 cm.) is reserved for each plant. Three hundred and eighty-three plant pictures (of originally 435) are preserved, which artistically fall easily into two groups: one quite naturalistic, surely copying an earlier, classical model very faithfully, and the other comparatively more abstract.

The picture of the violet (*viola odorosa*) belongs to the first group and excels, not only in its verisimilitude, but also in the graciousness and elegance of its design. Since it is a copy, this is all the more remarkable, in view of Pliny's realization (*Naturalis Historia* XXV. IV. 8) that "imperfection arises from the manifold hazards in the accuracy of copyists."

Moreover, one must be reminded that such plant pictures were neither made solely for aesthetic pleasure nor for a scientific record *per se*, but for the utilitarian purpose of a plant's recognition by the pharmacologist who administered it for medicinal purposes. The violet, as Dioscurides states, "has a cooling faculty . . . helps a burning stomach, and the inflammations of the eyes . . . and they say that the purple part of the flower . . . does help the epilepsies that are upon children."

PLATE 19

VIENNA DIOSCURIDES
fol. 391v   *Coral*

In the Vienna codex Dioscurides' herbal is followed by a fragment in hexameter of the *Carmen de viribus herbarum* which has been attributed to Rufus of Ephesus, the pharmacologist placed at the lower right of the second collected frontispiece (Plate 16). Of the sixteen plants described in this fragment, only one is illustrated in a sumptuous full-page miniature, the coral, also called sea oak or sea tree, which ancient science classified as a plant.

Instead of depicting it at the bottom of the sea, the illustrator, for full visibility, lets the coral grow out of the sea, or rather a pond with a few rocks in the foreground marking the shore. With its exuberant ramification giving the effect of a cobweb or a fine net, and its dynamic, flamelike design, the illustrator has fused naturalism and patternization in a balanced manner. Yet the coral is brown instead of red; this may be an indication that the artist did not copy from nature but depended on a model which was still deeply steeped in classical imagery. The pond is filled like an aquarium with a great variety of sea creatures, presupposing the artist's knowledge of a specialized treatise on fishes. From another source he copied the personification of the Sea with lobster claws in her hair. She points at the coral and, holding an oar, leans on a sea monster with the shape of the constellation Cetus, which may very well have been copied out of an astronomical treatise. The close association between science and poetry is thus indicated both textually, by the form of the hexameter, and pictorially, by mythological additions.

20

PLATE 20

VIENNA DIOSCURIDES
fol. 483v *Birds*

Another addition to the Vienna codex is a paraphrase of an ornithological treatise by a certain Dionysius, supposedly Dionysius of Philadelphia. This is the
oldest treatise of its kind with illustrations of birds, most of which are very
faithful in design and color and of high artistic merit. In the first two books of
the treatise, the birds are intercalated without frame or background into the
text columns, while those of the third book are collected on a full page and
arranged in a grid of twenty-four squares. This third book includes a didactic
hunting treatise dealing with those birds which one catches with lime-twig,
snare, net, and trap. Most of the birds on this page are easily identifiable, start-
ing with the ostrich, the bustard, probably a moor hen, the partridge, etc.
However some of them are not even mentioned in the paraphrase, and thus one
must conclude that the illustrations go back to an older, fuller treatise, which
some scholars believe to have been that of Alexander of Myndos.

One also finds an arrangement in a grid pattern on late antique floor mosaics
from Antioch and elsewhere, where this decorative system is particularly fitting.
But whether such collective pictures originated in a manuscript and were
adapted in this form by mosaicists, or whether the mosaicists invented them and
exercised an influence on book illumination, is hard to say. No doubt the Vienna
Dioscurides is, in all its parts, our best witness of a highly developed classical
tradition of excellent scientific illustrations.

21

PLATE 21

COTTON GENESIS
fol. 26v *Abraham & Angels*

Among the relatively well preserved fragments of the Cotton Genesis manuscript, after the fire in the Cotton Library in 1731, is one which illustrates Abraham arguing with the angels about saving Sodom and Gomorrah from destruc-
tion (Genesis 18:23–32). Dressed in a short white tunic and a red sash, not at
all like a patriarch in a long garment although he is white-haired, Abraham
approaches the angels with a wide stride and vivid gestures suggesting the
urgency of his argument. The nimbed angels stride forward to meet him but
with measured steps, in a more hieratic pose. Only the first of the original three
is fully preserved, dressed, as they surely all were, in a gold-striated tunic and
the imperial purple chlamys with golden tablion and red-purple shoes, comparable to the archangels in mosaic at San Vitale in Ravenna. Their straight outlines and flat bodies stress their uncorporeality in contrast to the undulated out-
line and plastic treatment of Abraham's figure. The mastery of more abstract
forms is fully revealed in the cone form of the mountain behind Abraham and
the blue and pink ribbons of sky, sharply separated from each other.

The miniature is preceded by two scenes with Abraham meeting the angels
at Mamre and followed by one in which Abraham, his argument having been
unsuccessful, leaves the angels. Thus it forms a link in the chain of narrative
scenes. It is significant that the mosaicist of San Marco who used this manuscript as a source copied only the Mamre scenes, which are more important than
this miniature.

PLATE 22

COTTON GENESIS
Bristol IVv   *Lot's House*

While normally the miniatures in this manuscript are placed within the one-column text written in a regular uncial script, for some more complex scenes the artist utilized a full page or near full page, as in this case where there are only five lines of writing at the top of the page. The miniature depicts the scene in which the Sodomites assault Lot with threatening gestures, demanding that he hand over to them the two men to whom Lot has given hospitality (Genesis 19:4–11). The artist has chosen the most dramatic moment, in which one of the two guests (they are angels), grasps Lot's wrist as he vividly argues with the Sodomites, and pulls him back into the house, whose open door is visible. The grasping arm is all that is left of this angel, and nothing remains of the other. In a narrow strip below, in what is actually a subsequent scene, the smiting of the Sodomites with blindness is depicted by two men who have fallen to the ground. By this formula the artist has tried to pictorialize the phrase "they wearied themselves to find the door."

For both main figures, Lot and the foremost Sodomite, the painter used the same colors—white for the long tunics and red for the mantles—whereas the Sodomite, seen from the back, wears brown and green garments. Most garments show striation of heavy gold lines, which is widely used throughout the manuscript, in a much more pronounced way than in the *Vergilius Vaticanus* and the *Quedlinburg Itala* (Plates 4, 5). The tendency to flatten and widen the bodies, which we noticed also in some miniatures of the Milan *Iliad* (Plates 8, 10), has become even stronger in the Cotton Genesis. The heads, with their low foreheads and burning eyes, remind one of the charioteers in the papyrus (Plate 6). In both features one recognizes Egyptian elements.

22

PLATE 23

VIENNA GENESIS
pict. 3 *Deluge*

Although most probably somewhat later in date than the Cotton Genesis, the Vienna miniatures have better preserved that mode of the classical style which relates to impressionism. This is particularly obvious in the picture of the Deluge (Genesis 7:17ff.), which completely fills the lower half of the page, that area of each page reserved for the illustration. The upper half contains the often shortened text, written in splendid silver uncials on purple ground.

The three-tiered ark in the center is half-swamped by the breaking waves, while heavy rain pours down from a narrow strip of sky. Two victims still alive and struggling and a third already dead are, to the extent they are above sea level, depicted in bright flesh colors, while all the others are submerged and ashen. The illustrator delights in showing the victims in different, sometimes daringly foreshortened poses: one lies on his back with legs drawn up tightly; another is shown tumbling over headfirst. To dramatize the struggle, some are rendered limp and dead while others, as the boy who embraces a woman at the right, still cling desperately to life.

The Vienna Genesis shares the allotment of a large picture area to the Deluge with the Ashburnham Pentateuch (Plate 45), which, however, is iconographically unrelated.

In this manuscript there are three distinct illuminators at work, each with a pupil; the first painter, who is responsible for the Deluge, has been called the "miniaturist."

PLATE 24

VIENNA GENESIS
pict. 13   *Rebecca & Eliezer*

The principle of continuous narrative, which dominates the Genesis cycle, is
most effectively used in the episode of Eliezer's meeting with Rebecca. This
story, told in the first half of chapter 24, is illustrated in no fewer than eight
scenes distributed over three miniatures, each having two superimposed zones.
In the first miniature, Eliezer is sent off by Abraham, leaves with ten camels,
and arrives at the well outside the city of Nahor; in the second, Rebecca
appears and offers water to him; and in the third Eliezer gazes at Rebecca, gives
her a ring and then she talks to her parents in their house.

Whereas the first and third miniatures keep the two zones separate, in the
second the artist tries to combine them into one plane. Rebecca, clad in a pink
robe, has just left the city of Nahor, a typical Hellenistic walled city, and walks
downhill along a colonnaded street which makes a hairpin turn. At the bend a
half-naked nymph, her legs covered by a purple garment, is leaning in antique
fashion on a water urn. The water from the urn flows into a river from which
Rebecca has drawn water, filling a trough. In a very realistic pose she rests one
foot on the rim of the trough and gives Eliezer, who "ran to meet her," a drink
from the same water jar she carries upon her shoulder in the upper scene. The
eager Eliezer is followed by his ten camels, likewise eager to drink. This miniature, attributed also to the "miniaturist," has a bucolic charm, deeply rooted in
the classical tradition.

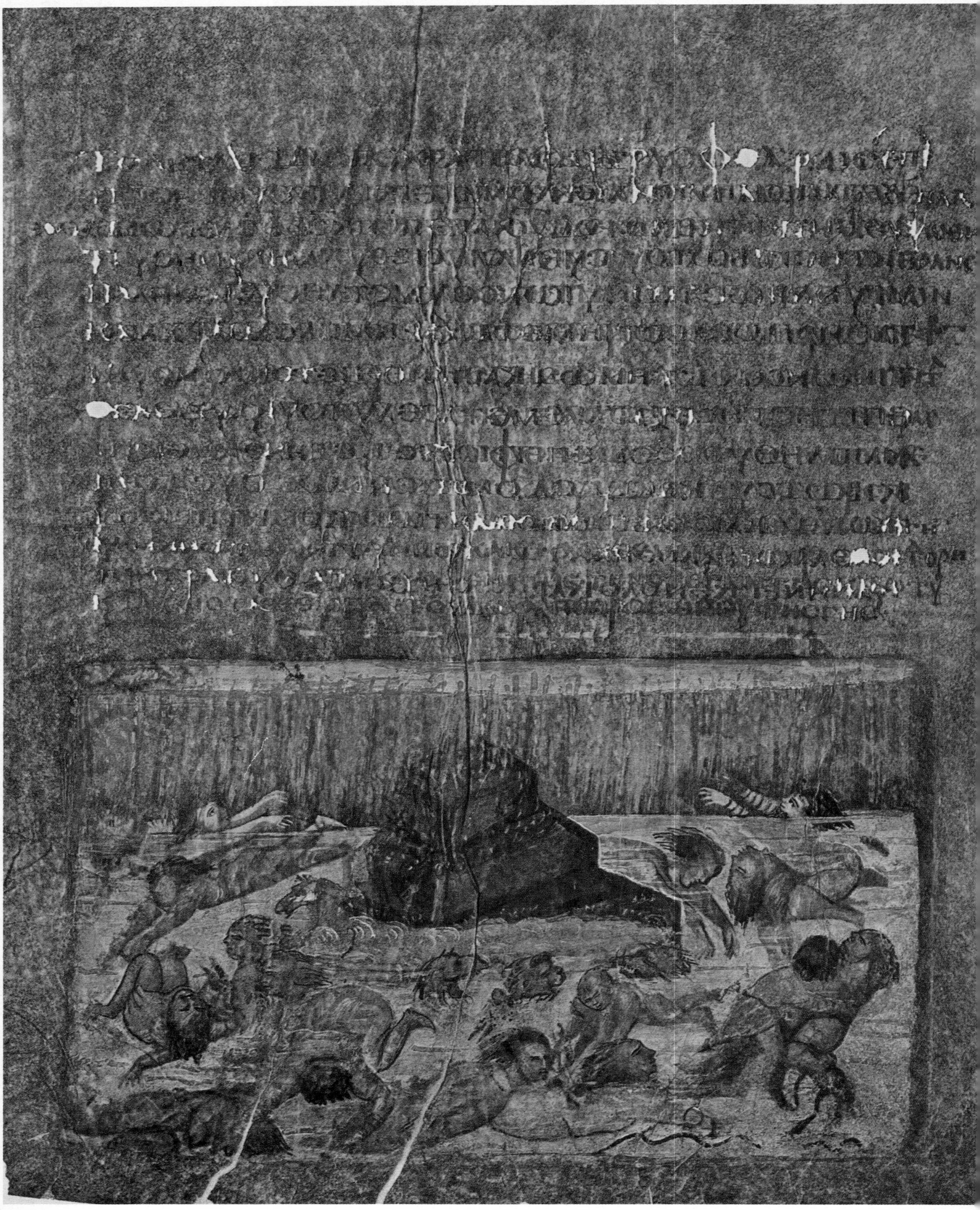

23

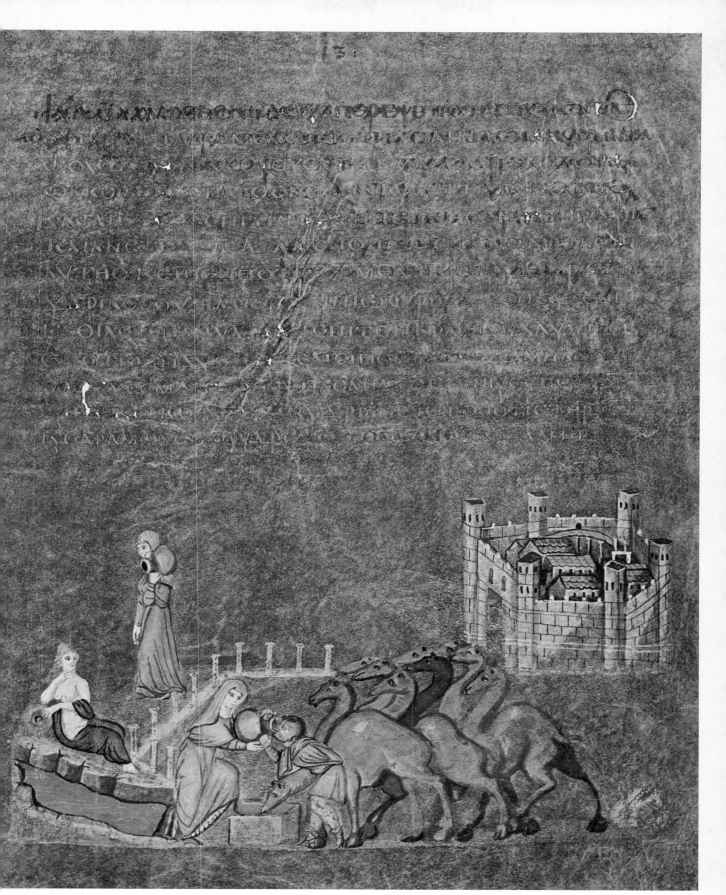

PLATE 25

V I E N N A G E N E S I S
pict. 30 *Joseph's Departure*

As in literature the Joseph story has often been paraphrased and expanded with legendary detail, so too has the illustrator of the Vienna Genesis enriched the extensive Joseph cycle by extraneous elements which are not contained in the Bible text. Many of these elements have recently been explained by Jewish legends, and the assumption has been made that they derive from Jewish book illumination, since the synagogue of Dura has proved the existence of Jewish representational arts as early as the third century.

The episode of Joseph being sent to Shechem (Genesis 37:14ff.) is depicted in four scenes, each filling a quarter of the surface area. In the first, Joseph's farewell is rendered with charming intimacy: he bends down to kiss the little Benjamin farewell, while Jacob, seated in an easy chair, tenderly touches Joseph's chin. The woman behind Joseph is not explained by the Bible, and while some have interpreted her as Leah, more likely she is "Bilhah, Rachel's housemaid who had brought him [Joseph] up like a mother," as told in the *Midrashim*. As he departs, Joseph turns around to the weeping Benjamin, while he is led off by an angel. This angel, not explained by the Bible, can be identified as Gabriel, according to the *Pirke* of Rabbi Eliezer. Then follows a scene in which, close to the Bible text, a man seen from the back points out to Joseph the way to Dothan where his brothers had moved, and finally, with the figure scale much reduced and separated from the last scene by a rock, we see Joseph within sight of his brothers, who point excitedly at him. In front of Joseph is a dog, explainable once more by a *Midrash*, "Let us kill him by inciting dogs against him." At the same time, the little church on top of the hill is a distinctly Christian feature. Here we have a product of the second artist, termed the "colorist."

ΚΤ ΗΔΙΚΑ ΠΟΡΕΥΘΟCΟΜΔΕCΥΠΡΑΥΘΕΝΟΝΕΧ
ΦΟΙCΟΥΚΑΙΤΑΠΡΟΒΑΤΑΚΑΙΑΜΑΤΙΛΟΚΑΙΠΙΚΑΙ
ΧΠΕCΤΙΛΕΝΑΥΤΟΝΕΚΤΗCΚΟΙΛΛΟCΤΗCΧΟΛΙ
ΕΧΛΗΝΔΟΕΝΕΙCΟΥΧΕΜΤΧΙΕΥΡΕΝΑΥΤΟΝΙΝΙΕΖΑΜ
ΕΙΠΟΜΕΝΟΝΕΝΤΟΠΕΔΙΟΕΡΦΗCΟΜΚΑΙΠΙΑ
ΑΟΑΝΘΡΩΠΟCΛΕΓΩΝΤΙΖΗΤΕΙCΟΔΕΕΙΠΕΝΑΥΤΩ
ΤΟΥCΑΔΕΛΦΟΥCΜΟΥΖΗΤΩΑΝΑΠΑΓΓΕΙΛΟΝ
ΒΟΕΚΟΥΟΤΗΕΙΠΕΝΔΕΑΥΤΩ ΟΧΝΟΔΑΠΕΡΚΑΙ
ΕΝΤΕΥΘΕΝΗΚΟΥCΑΓΑΧΥΤΟΝΛΕΓΟΝΤΩΝ
ΡΕΥΘΩΜΕΝΕΙCΧΟΘΕΙΑΙΚΑΙΕΠΟΡΕΥΘΗΕCΟΗ
ΚΑΤΟΠΙCΘΕΝΤΩΝΧΑΔΕΧΦΟΝΑΥΤΟΥΚΑΙΕΟ
ΑΥΤΟΥCΕΝΔΟΘΕΙΜ ΠΡΟΕΙΛΟΝΑΞΕΜΙCΟΝΟΙΤΑ
ΘΕΝΠΡΟΤΟΥΕΓΓΙCΑΠΡΟCΑΥΤΟΥCΗ CΟΘΙ
ΟΝΤΟΤΟΥΑΠΟΚΤΙΝΑΙΤΟΝΕΝΟΛΙΔΕΕΙΓΧΟΕ

ΑΠΕΧΕΙ ΟΥΔΕΝ ΠΛΗΝ ΣΟΥ ΔΙΑ ΤΟ ΣΕ ΓΥΝΑΙΚΑ ΑΥΤ
ΕΙΝΑΙ ΚΑΙ ΠΩΣ ΠΟΙΗΣΩ ΤΟ ΡΗΜΑ ΤΟ ΠΟΝΗΡΟ
ΤΟΥΤΟ ΚΑΙ ΑΜΑΡΤΗΣΟΜΑΙ ΕΝΑΝΤΙΟΝ ΤΟΥ ΘΥ
ΗΝΙΚΑ ΕΛΑΛΕΙ ΤΩ ΙΩΣΗΦ ΗΜΕΡΑΝ ΕΞ ΗΜΕΡΑΣ
ΚΑΙ ΟΥΧ ΥΠΗΚΟΥΣΕΝ ΑΥΤΗ ΚΑΘΕΥΔΕΙΝ ΜΕΤΑ
ΤΟΥ ΣΥΝΓΕΝΕΣΘΑΙ ΑΥΤΗ ΕΓΕΝΕΤΟ ΔΕ ΤΟΙΑΥΤ
ΤΙΩ ΗΜΕΡΑ ΕΙΣΗΛΘΕΝ ΙΩΣΗΦ ΕΙΣ ΤΗΝ ΟΙΚΙΑΝ
ΠΟΙΕΙΝ ΤΑ ΕΡΓΑ ΑΥΤΟΥ ΚΑΙ ΟΥΘΕΙΣ ΤΩΝ ΕΝ ΤΗ
ΟΙΚΙΑ ΕΣΩ ΕΠΕΣΠΑΣΑΤΟ ΑΥΤΟΝ ΤΩΝ ΙΜΑΤΙ
ΛΕΓΟΥΣΑ ΚΟΙΜΗΘΗΤΙ ΜΕΤ ΕΜΟΥ ΚΑΙ ΚΑΤΑΛΙΠ
ΤΑ ΙΜΑΤΙΑ ΕΝ ΤΑΙΣ ΧΕΡΣΙΝ ΑΥΤΗΣ ΕΦΥΓΕΝ ΚΣ
ΕΞΗΛΘΕΝ ΕΞΩ ΚΑΙ ΕΓΕΝΕΤΟ ΩΣ ΕΙΔΕΝ ΟΤΙ
ΚΑΤΑΛΙΠΩΝ ΤΑ ΙΜΑΤΙΑ ΑΥΤΟΥ ΕΝ ΤΑΙΣ ΧΕΡΣΙΝ Α
ΥΤΗΣ ΚΑΙ ΕΦΥΓΕΝ ΚΑΙ ΕΞΗΛΘΕΝ ΕΞΩ ΕΚΑΛΕΣΕ

PLATE 26

Vienna Genesis
pict. 31 *Temptation of Joseph*

After a gap of six missing folios, with twelve miniatures and twice or three times as many scenes, the Joseph story continues with the episode of his temptation by Potiphar's wife (Genesis 39:11ff.). Dressed in a transparent garment, the temptress sits on the edge of a gilded bed before a double-rowed colonnade, suggesting a stately palace chamber; she grasps the edge of Joseph's purple mantle, which he tries to slip out of. Next Joseph is repeated looking back at the open door through which he has just escaped. To this point the illustration is biblical, but the rest in the upper zone and all of the lower are additions which once were regarded as "novelistic," but which, in light of the preceding miniature, must be interpreted as features of Jewish legends, although in this particular case a satisfactory explanation has yet to be offered. Here a wide area for future research has just been opened.

The figure at the top right in a star-studded mantle and holding a spindle has been explained as an astrologer, and the woman bending over the cradle once more as Potiphar's wife, holding a rattle over a baby which, on the basis of Jewish sources, has been thought to be Osnath (Asenath in Greek), an adopted daughter whom Joseph is later to marry. Even less surely identified are the figures in the lower register, a woman holding a naked baby and two seated women spinning, the one at the right clad like Potiphar's wife in the first scene in a transparent garment. Only the two trees can be dismissed as "space fillers."

This miniature also is a work of the "colorist," who successfully displays his painterly qualities in the transparent garments. The swaying pose of the woman holding the child has parallels in contemporary mosaics from Antioch.

ΕΚΤΟΥ...
ΠΛΛΕΚΗΙϹ...
ΔϹΠΛΛΛΕΛΕΛ...
ΚΛΡΛΛΕΝΘΦ...
...

PLATE 27

VIENNA GENESIS
pict. 33 *Joseph in Prison*

After another interruption of missing leaves, we next see Joseph in prison inter-
preting the dreams of the baker and the butler (Genesis 40:9ff.)—a scene
apparently considered so important that the artist has utilized the whole picture
area for it. Joseph sits in the middle giving the bad news to the baker, who
makes a gesture of sorrow or despair, while the butler stretches his arms
towards heaven in gratitude for his impending liberation. The prison is rendered like an open court, into which one looks in bird's-eye view. Outside the
prison and before a sundial sits the guard, who turns around to a woman who
has approached him from behind and apparently is entreating him. She cannot
be explained by the Bible text, but in a *Midrash* we find the legend that Potiphar's wife, here named Zuleika, had persuaded her husband not to kill Joseph
so she could continue to pursue him, even while he was in prison. That Potiphar's wife is depicted in rather somber garments, a brown tunic and purplish
paenula, is easily enough explained by her desire to look inconspicuous during
these escapades.

   This miniature is typical of the style of the third master, who has been
termed the "illusionist," and with good reason. The quick brush technique used
for the trees behind the prison wall comes particularly close to an impressionistic technique.

ΡΥΟΜΕΝΟϹΜΟΕΓΙϹΑΝΤΩΝΤΟΝΙΝΧΓΓϹϹΩΝΙϹΥΝΟΡΗ
ΤΑΙΓΑΔΙΑΤΑΥΤΑΚΑΙΕϹΗΚΛΩΘΗϹΕΤΕΘΕΜΗΥΤ
ΟϹΖΥΜΤΕΙϹΗΓΡΟΝΑΒΡΑΑΜΚΑΙϹΑΑΚΚΑΙΗΠΕΤΟΥ
ΠΑΚΟΥΙΖΩΝΙϹΑΝΕΙϹΑΝΒΟϹΠΟΛΥΕΠΙΤΗϹΓΗΡΟΙ
ΖΛΙΙΙΤΑΕΙϹΘΕΝΦΟΤΙΕΡΕΒΑϹΕΝΟΠΗΡΑΥΤΟΥΤΩΝ
ΧΩΥϹΟΠΙΜΠΛΑΕΞΙΧΛΑΥΤΟΥΕΠΙΤΗΝΚΕΦΑΛΗΝΕΦΡΕΜ
ΝΗΥΤΕϹΦΑΝΗΗΚΑΙΕΠΕΛΛΒΕΤΟΙϹΦΚΗΖΟΕ
ΡΟΥΥΠΡΟΑΥΤΟΥΧΙΓΕΛΕΙΠΛΑΥΤΗΝΑΠΟΤΗϹΚΕΦΑΛΗϹ
ΡΕΜΕΝΟΠΙΤΗϹΧΖΖΛΙΝΧΜΑΝΙΥΟϹΗΣΕΠΕΛΛΕ
ΙΔΩΝΦΤΟΠΡΑΥΤΟΥΟΥΧΟΥΤΩϹΙΕΡΟΥΤΟϹϹΕΖ
ΠΡΩΠΟΤΟΚΟϹϹΕΠΙΟϹΤΗΧΕΡΑΤΗΝΔΕΖΙΜΑΥ
ΛΠΟΤΗΝΚΕΦΑΛΗΝΑΥΤΟΑΚΧΛΟΥΚΗΘΟϹΗΜΝΩΛΛΑ
ΟΤΟϹΩΓΛΕΓΝΟΜΗ ΠΕΑΙϹΚΟΥϹΟϹϹΕΘΕΙϹ
ΝΙΛΟΥΤΟϹ ΤΖΜ ΙΧΟϹΧΟΙΔΕΦΘϹΠΥ
ΜΤΩ ΩΕΡΕ ϹΑΝΖϹΟΠΛΥΠΟΥϹΟϹΙϹϹΩΝΟΠΕΡΩΙ

PLATE 28

V I E N N A G E N E S I S
pict. 45 *Blessing of Ephraim & Manasseh*

The Blessing of Ephraim and Manasseh (Genesis 48:13ff.) is depicted as the
only scene on this page, in a monumental figure scale, showing the nearly blind
patriarch Jacob seated on a throne, placing his right hand on the younger
Ephraim and his left on the older Manasseh. Joseph, dressed in a tunic and the
imperial purple chlamys with golden tablion and wearing the golden torque
which Pharaoh had given him, attempts to correct Jacob's action by trying to
remove his left hand from Manasseh's head so that he can be blessed properly
with the right hand. The miniature thus depicts the moment after the actual
blessing, which quite likely was depicted in the preceding miniature, now lost.
Behind Joseph stands his Egyptian wife, Asenath. She is not mentioned in the
Bible; we have here another of the many legendary additions typical of the
Joseph story.

   Although very competent in his use of color, the "illusionist," to whom this
miniature is attributed, shows a considerable weakness in the structure of the
bodies, compared with both the "miniaturist" and the "colorist." The over-sized
heads contrast with the spindly legs, and the two boys are rendered in swaying
poses, so as to fit, together with Jacob, into a triangular pattern.

   One would expect such a scene to take place inside a house, and in other
Genesis cycles this scene indeed has an architectural setting. Our artist, however, set the scene in a luminous landscape. The mountains changing from
green to brown, and the pink sky turning to light and dark blue, show his mastery of an impressionistic technique.

PLATE 29

ROSSANO GOSPELS
fol. 1r *Raising of Lazarus*

The first of the full-page miniatures in the purple Gospels of Rossano depicts the Raising of Lazarus in all its details as told in the Gospel of John. The sisters of Lazarus have prostrated themselves before Christ, who is surrounded by Apostles and townspeople; next to the body of Lazarus, wrapped like a mummy in the open tomb, stands a servant, his nose covered up in a very realistic rendering of the phrase "by this time he [Lazarus] stinketh" (John 11:39). Underneath stand two pairs of prophets, David and Hosea and David and Isaiah, holding open scrolls with quotations from their writings alluding to the New Testament events.

The two parts of the miniature must be viewed as a whole and be explained by liturgical usage, according to which a passage from the Psalter precedes the lesson of the day, in this case the reading for the Saturday before Palm Sunday. Such a composition was surely not invented for a Gospel Book but reflects monumental wall painting in which a series of selected scenes from the New Testament is aligned in an upper row and prophets with their open scrolls in the lower, an arrangement of which the frescoes in Sant' Angelo in Formis, where the prophets stand in the spandrels of an arcade, are a striking example. It most likely is also due to the influence of monumental painting that the composition is so rich in bystanders, since a normal Gospel scene in a large narrative cycle would be more restricted to the essential figures.

The artist delights in expressive poses and movement—the quick advance of Christ, the vivid gestures of some bystanders, and especially the pointing prophets. Among the vividly colored dresses, the golden mantle of Christ stands out for its hieratic and dematerialized quality.

ΑΚΩΝΔΕΠΙΛΑΤΟCΟΤΙΕΚΤΗCΕΞΟΥCΙΑCΗΡΩΑΟΥΕCΤΙΝΑΝΕΠΕΜΨΕΝΑΥΤΟ
ΡΟCΗΡΩΑΗΝΟΝΤΑΚΛΛΥΤΟΝΕΝΙΕΡΟCΟΛΥΜΟΙCΕΝΤΑΥΤΛΙCΤΑΙCΗΜΕΡΑΙC
ΚΗCΛΝΤΕCΛΥ ΔΙΛΕΙ
ΓΛΟΙΝΤΕCΔΛΛΛΗΛω
ΡΗ ΘωΥΝΤΛΛΙΠ
ΙΗΝΜ

ΒΑΡΑΒ
ΒΛC

ΛΛΑΤΙΝΗΠ ΙΛΛΤΟCΛΕCΤΙΚΑΤΑΕΙΡΗΝΗΛΝΕΤΟΙΑΛΛΗΝΘΡΟΙCΙΤΟΔΙCΛΥΘΛCΝΗωΔΙΑΤ
ΤΛΙΟ ΙΙΟΗΟΛΑΜΗΓΙΝΟΛΛΦΡΛΟΤΗΝΟΤΛΛΜΗΝΙωΜΕΙΝΙΥCΥΘΒΙΧΟΟΙΟΥ
ΕΠΙΑΗΝΟΠΟΛΙΛΝ ΙCΛΝΙΚΟΛΝΕΙCΗΙΤ

31

PLATE 30

R O S S A N O   G O S P E L S
fol. 8r   *Christ Before Pilate*

Two miniatures of the Rossano Gospels are distinct from all others: they are scenic illustrations filling the entire page and terminating in a semicircle. Similarly composed, they are obviously companion pieces depicting in a hieratic manner befitting the dignity of the imperial court the trial before Pilate. In the center, high on a throne, sits Pilate behind a table of juridical importance. Not like a villain but as the *dux consularis* of Palestine, radiating authority, he looks thoughtfully at the silent Christ who has just entered the courtroom with the high priests Annas and Caiaphas. The group at the left is balanced by a group of court officials standing stiffly at the right. The very essence of the picture is the expurgation of Pilate, implying that the blame is to be laid with the high priests.

In contrast to this ceremonial composition are the two narrative scenes below, in which Judas returns the thirty pieces of silver to the two high priests as Annas, the older one, makes a spontaneous gesture of abhorrence. Then Judas hangs himself.

The Pilate scene is clearly inspired by an imperial court scene and adjusted to the Gospel narrative. The circumscribed arc suggests a dependence on a niche composition, a monumental model either in fresco or mosaic.

The artist was quite capable of casting his monumental model into the mode of a miniaturist. The soft modeling of the figures of Pilate and the high priests, with their clinging mantles, contrasts with the flat chlamides of the court officials and especially with the gold mantle of Christ. Also typical of the style of the Rossano Gospels are the orientalizing heads of some figures that one associates with the Greco-Syrian style of this period.

PLATE 31

R O S S A N O   G O S P E L S
fol. 8v   *Christ Before Pilate*

The second picture of the trial before Pilate, although likewise divided into two strips, nevertheless depicts a single scene. Pilate, seen in the same dignified pose, is flanked by dense groups of Jews who gesture wildly and shout: "Away with this man and release unto us Barabbas." The murderer Barabbas, clad only in a loincloth and fettered, is brought before Pilate by two guards, while Christ, in a most dignified pose, is flanked by two court officials, one holding "green shoots," a scepter-like symbol alluding to his kingship.

This miniature too has strongly maintained the character of a monumental composition. The manner in which the shouting Jews press against the semicircular line, the farther ones suspended, suggests that in this case the model was not a simple niche, but an apse. It has been convincingly argued that the Praetorium, the hall in which the actual judgment of Pilate took place, and which was included already in the oldest description of the holy places of Jerusalem by the pilgrim of Bordeaux (333 A.D.), had monumental scenes of the Pilate story.

If we place the composition of this miniature in an apse, it seems likely that the two lower groups were separated by an apse window, in which case the one guard looking upward would be placed more to the right to meet the eyes of Pilate. The previous miniature, then, was most likely a niche to the left, requiring another niche to the right, whose most logical subject would have been Pilate washing his hands.

PLATE 32

ROSSANO GOSPELS
fol. 7v *Good Samaritan*

One of the important Sunday readings is the passage Luke 10:75ff. with the parable of the Good Samaritan. From a more extensive narrative cycle, as seen in some Gospel Books, the artist has chosen only the two phases which center on the Samaritan, rather than on the man who has been beaten. It is peculiar to the painter of this manuscript that he interprets the Samaritan as Christ himself. In the dominating central scene, Christ bends over the beaten man and tends to his wounds, assisted by an angel who holds a bowl with veiled hands, just as in the Baptism angels reverently hold Christ's garments. The inspiration may well come from a Baptism scene striving for a similar hieratic effect and stressing the liturgical. The second scene, in which Christ, followed by the wounded man riding on an ass, pays the innkeeper, is of a more purely narrative character and is compositionally balanced by the city of Jericho at the left. Once more we see two pairs of prophets below, in this instance David and Micah and David and Sirach.

The story of the Good Samaritan is not the only parable depicted in the Rossano Gospels, which also has a miniature of the Wise and Foolish Virgins, another Sunday lesson within the liturgical cycle.

PLATE 33

ROSSANO GOSPELS
fol. 121r *Saint Mark*

It is an indication of the losses of Early Christian book illumination that of the most often represented subject, the portraits of the Evangelists, only one single Greek example has come down to us—that of Mark in the Rossano Gospels. The Evangelist, sitting in a wicker chair, writes the beginning of his Gospel in the old fashioned manner, in a scroll instead of a codex, suggesting an early model. Before him stands a nimbed woman in a long blue robe and veil, dictating to and inspiring him.

The composition ultimately goes back to that of an ancient poet or philosopher inspired by a Muse, but in the Christian adaptation, the contemplating figure becomes a busy Gospel writer and the Muse a personification—in this case not identified, but in later Christian examples inscribed "Sophia."

The group has a background and a frame which are not quite correlated. The former consists of a blue wall surmounted by a huge square from which draperies flow down to the corners of the wall. This is a highly abstract form of the precinct wall of a sacred grove, as seen in Pompeian frescoes, with a projecting gate from which such draperies sprawl. The color formula behind the draperies, pink to light blue to blue, is reminiscent of the sunset. The outer frame, likewise highly abstracted, is to be derived from the center of a *porta regia* of the Roman theater. Its distinctive features are the colored marble columns with golden rings to hold back curtains, and the conch atop the entablature.

In this Greco-Syrian miniature, very markedly different from the Constantinopolitan miniature of the Dioscurides portrait (Plate 17), more than in any of the figurative scenes the distance from the classical past and the development of a more abstract style are apparent.

PLATE 34

RABBULA GOSPELS
fol. 4v *Canon Table*

The third of this unusually large set of nineteen Canon Tables consists, like all the others, of very slender, dematerialized and ornate columns, supporting a lunette and enclosing the numerals of the Eusebian concordance, in this case the end of the first Canon with the parallels of all four Gospels. In the margins are scenes from a New Testament cycle illustrating the events of Christ's life in a harmonized way, just as textually the Four Gospels were harmonized in Tatian's *Diatesseron.*

The scene of the Nativity shows the Virgin seated before the manger in the form of a block altar upon which the Christ child lies; Joseph bends over the child from behind. The background is reminiscent of the cave turned into a sanctuary as it existed in the Nativity Church, and thus the representation is a *locus sanctus* picture from Bethlehem. Omitting the Adoration, we see underneath the Nativity, distributed over both margins, the Massacre of the Innocents in which Herod is rendered in an extremely agitated pose, and at the left the Baptism of Christ with the strange feature of what has been described as a yellow flame emanating from the Jordan, an allusion to Luke 3:16, "I shall baptize you with the Holy Ghost and with fire." In the upper spandrels, appropriate to the Nativity, are two of the royal ancestors of Christ, David and Solomon, both clad in the purple chlamys with golden tablion like Byzantine emperors: David, standing frontally, holds the lyre, and Solomon, seated on a very elaborate throne and holding a globe, is apparently an adaptation of a Christ type.

34

PLATE 35

RABBULA GOSPELS
fol. 9v   *Matthew & John*

After Canon V, the New Testament cycle adorning the margins is interrupted
for the four Evangelists, accompanying Canons VI and VII. The Evangelists
are too important to be relegated to the margins, and the artist has placed them
into architectural settings which replace the outer columns of the Canon
Tables. They are a mixture of two types: two are seated under elaborate struc-
tures, and two are standing holding codices under very simple architectural
frames.

The elderly Matthew is seated at the right in an almost frontal pose, raising
his right hand in a gesture of speech as if addressing an audience, while in his
lap rests his Gospel, not firmly held and seeming to slide down, indicating that
it may have been added by the copyist, working from a model without it. The
youthful John at the left sits on a high-backed folding chair reading a vertically
unrolled scroll, a burning lamp on a slender stand giving him light. It will be
noticed that, contrary to Mark in the Rossano Gospels (Plate 33), Matthew
and John are not engaged in writing, but in teaching and reading. In this they
still reflect more closely the types of ancient philosophers and poets from which
they are ultimately derived. Statues of seated poets were often connected in
ancient art with the *scenae frons* of the theater, and this explains the architectural setting in our miniature: the structure around Matthew is reminiscent of
the *tempietto* in the center of the *scenae frons,* and the conch above John, as in
the Mark picture of the Rossano Gospels, is also a motif to be derived from this
source.

PLATE 36

R A B B U L A   G O S P E L S
fol. 13v   *Ascension*

Like the Rossano Gospels, the Rabbula manuscript has several full-page miniatures which, because of their complexity, are not simple narrative illustrations,
but clearly reflect monumental compositions. The imposing composition of the
Ascension contains many elements which cannot be explained by the text of
the Acts of the Apostles but were chosen for dogmatic reasons. The Virgin,
dressed in purple, stands isolated in the pose of an Orant. Not present in the
biblical narrative, she is introduced here as guarantee of the humanity of
Christ, who had come down to earth through her. Likewise alluding to the
human nature of Christ are the two angels offering crowns with veiled hands,
an allusion to Hebrews 2:7, "Thou madest him a little lower than the angels;
thou crownest him with glory and honour." Paul himself, whose presence in
this picture is also unjustified by the text, seems to explain this passage by holding a codex slightly opened with one finger and pointing to the ascending
Christ. The third extraneous element is the tetramorph and firewheels based on
various visions of Ezekiel. The picture must be understood as a glorification of
the dogma of the Two Natures of Christ as formulated at the council of Chalcedon in 451. One can only speculate that such a composition was invented for
the church on the Mount of Olives where the Ascension had taken place. The
frame, suggesting *tesserae*, may be an indication that the model was a mosaic.
Such a model, from a somewhat earlier period, must indeed have been very
much in the tradition of a Hellenistic painterly style with an impressionistic
landscape comparable to those in the Vienna Genesis (Plate 28). Only in the
human figures, with their slightly exaggerated undulated outlines, the vivid
gesturing, and the vehement movements of the angels, does a Syrian element
seem to have penetrated the powerful Greek tradition.

PLATE 37

R ABBULA G OSPELS
fol. 14r   *Christ Enthroned*

Another miniature derived from a monumental model, in this case surely an apse, shows Christ enthroned against a blue mandorla and flanked by two white-haired ecclesiastics, perhaps saints (although they have no nimbi), one of whom wears a monk's hood. They present two younger men to Christ, in a grouping similar to that of the well-known mosaic of Cosma and Damiano in Rome, where Peter and Paul lead the two title saints to Christ. In our miniature, all four wear the somber, brown garments which one associates with monks, although the pallium worn by the three bareheaded figures is not particularly a monk's dress.

Unfortunately these figures are not inscribed, and their identification is, therefore, unsure. For the monk, the name of Ephraim the Syrian has been proposed, but this is hardly more than a suggestion. Since several of the full-page miniatures in the Rabbula Gospels can be associated with holy sites in Jerusalem, this raises the question whether the apse reflected in the miniature goes back to a Jerusalem church, in which case the monk could just as well have been a Greek, perhaps Euthymios, or another Palestinian.

Only the five figures should be associated with the monumental model, and they may have been adapted to the special needs of a manuscript dedication picture by the addition of codices to the hands of two of them. Moreover, the green background with blue trees, and especially the arch similar to those used for Canon Tables—more specifically the Eusebius letter preceding them—are decorative elements in the miniature tradition.

PLATE 38

RABBULA GOSPELS
fol. 14v *Pentecost*

The next full-page miniature also reflects a monumental composition, apparently of a niche casting a shadow. Depicted is a very unusual Pentecost, with the Apostles not seated in a circle or semicircle, but standing flanking the Virgin who, as in the Ascension picture, is not called for by the text of the Acts. Yet these two Virgin types are quite different, the one in the Pentecost being less corporeal and more abstract. This may be due in part to different hands, but even more to models from two different periods, that of the Pentecost seemingly the later one.

The iconography is unique in that the Virgin is not, as usual, flanked by Peter and Paul, who cannot even be identified with certainty. To her right stands most prominently an apostle with a sparse white beard, who must be identified as James, the brother of the Lord, "the oldest among them," and the first Bishop of Jerusalem.

There was in Jerusalem in the church of Sion, the patriarchal Church, a chapel of the Holy Spirit thought to be the place of the actual event. This chapel had, at least as early as the crusader period, a mosaic of the Pentecost, and it seems quite likely that our miniature reflects this lost mosaic.

Stylistically the miniature represents the most advanced style, already moving away from the classical tradition. The figures are rendered in a summary fashion, with a tubular effect, and in this a Syrian element asserts itself. The same is true for the heads: that at the extreme left betrays oriental features such as were found also in the Vienna Genesis and Rossano Gospels (Plates 28 and 29).

38

PLATE 39

THE SYRIAC BIBLE OF PARIS
fol. 46r *Job*

In a few cases the artist of this Bible has placed at the head of an individual book, instead of a standing author, a scenic representation. It is not by chance that one of these is from the Book of Job; next to the Psalter Job is the most often illustrated Old Testament book in the East. There are no fewer than fifteen copies preserved, which begin with the prolific illustration of the first two chapters. Such a model has been excerpted by our illustrator, who, to give as much as possible of the narrative, fused elements of several scenes around the naked Job, covered with sores and reclining on a dungheap. First, his despondent wife sits at the lower right, having a discourse with him before his three friends appear (Job 2:9). Then one of the three friends, excerpted from the scene of their arrival, upon seeing the great sufferer in distress, rends his garment (Job 2:12); and finally we see two of the three friends sitting and beginning the conversations which form the core of the book (Job 2:13). At the upper left is Job's house, perhaps a remnant from still an earlier scene before his many misfortunes.

It is significant that, with perhaps two exceptions, the illustrated Job manuscripts are all products of the East Byzantine provinces, and the special importance of the Book of Job in the Syrian Bible is that it immediately follows the Pentateuch.

Although rather summary in his brush technique, the illustrator has quite skillfully composed a harmonious semicircular grouping of the various elements with no rifts resulting from the process of conflation. The landscape setting, with pink and blue sky, still reveals the painterly classical tradition.

PLATE 40

T H E S Y R I A C B I B L E O F P A R I S
fol. 8r   *Moses Before Pharaoh*

The miniature to the book of Genesis, which might have been more sumptuous than any other, is lost; the first picture in this manuscript belongs to the beginning of Exodus. Why the artist should have chosen out of a narrative cycle the scene in which Moses and Aaron ask Pharaoh for permission to leave the country is hardly understandable, since other subjects from Exodus were more popular.

Moses approaches hastily with a wide step and raises his right hand accusingly against Pharaoh, who, holding his scepter menacingly in his left hand, seems angered and about to jump up from his throne. In contrast to the excited protagonists, Aaron, holding the budding rod as his attribute, stands in a stiff frontal pose behind Moses, as do the bodyguards behind Pharaoh. To depict the

PLATE 40 (Continued)

ruler dressed in the imperial purple chlamys in such an agitated pose is quite against the *raison et mesure* of Constantinopolitan art but seems typical of Syrian art; in the scene of the Massacre of the Innocents in the Rabbula Gospels we saw Herod in a very similar pose, seemingly jumping up from his throne (Plate 34).

In style the illustrator followed the Rabbula Gospels closely, especially the painter of the Pentecost picture (Plate 38). The figure of Moses, with the garment wrapped around a cylindrical body, and the fluffy brush technique visible in the heads, may particularly be compared with the Apostles of the Pentecost. It thus seems that this Bible cannot be dated much later than the Rabbula Gospels, and may belong to the sixth or perhaps the early seventh century.

ܩܘܩܝܘ ܗܦܟܬ ܕܐܝܡ ܕܐܬܝ ܟܦܘܠܬܐ
ܘܥܠܡ ܟܘܪܒܐ ܕܝܬ ܡܐܢܬܟ
ܕܒܠܐ ܠܥܡܪ̈ܝܢ ܚܠܡ ܢܚܙܦܬܐ. ܚܒܖ
ܘܗܘܬ ܥܠܐ. ܕܐܚܠܟ ܡܥܡܕܗܝ
ܘܠܘܢ ܘܬܘܡ ܡܥܒܬܥܚܕ ܘܐܚܕܠܟ.

ܠܥܒܐܕ ܘܠܪܙܡܘܣܗ ܘܓܒܕ
ܘܗܠܡ ܡܥܟܕܝܡ ܗܘܘ   ܠܘܡ.
ܬܚܙܠܐ ܚܠܝܢ ܗܘܘ ܘܚܘܚܕܐ ܠܐܒܥ
ܗܘܘ. ܡܟܚܠܐ ܠܗܘܡ ܡܢ   ܡܕܝܡ
ܬܚ ܠܐܒܥܕܠܟ. ܘܡܥܟܬܚܕܗ ܗܘܘ

PLATE 41

THE GOSPELS OF SAINT AUGUSTINE
fol. 125r   *New Testament Scenes*

Preceding the Gospel of Luke is a collective miniature in twelve scenes covering the early phase of Christ's Passion, from the Entry into Jerusalem to Symon
of Cyrene carrying the cross. These are not all taken from Luke's Gospel, but we
deal here—just as in the Rabbula Gospels (Plate 34)—with a harmonized cycle
from all four Gospels. A similar page before John's Gospel, now lost, must
have similarly illustrated the end of the Passion and the events following it;
scenes from the early life of Christ supposedly came before Matthew's and
Mark's Gospels.

In collecting scenes originally strewn into the Gospel text, the illustrator was
obviously hard pressed for space and resorted to omissions (showing only eight
Apostles at the Last Supper), and occasionally to cutting figures off at the
margin. The stocky proportions of the figures, the simply designed garments
and expressionless faces, reveal that the artist is more interested in the decorative distribution of the compositional elements (note the abstract colors of the
hilly background) than in the organic structure of the human body. In this he
foreshadows Western development. There are also Western features in the
iconography, for example, Christ riding astride the donkey in the Entry. Having
Peter in the Washing of the Feet seated on a high-backed throne seems a specifically Roman touch.

Although essentially narrative, the impact of liturgical imagery can be seen
in the upper center in the scenes of the Last Supper and the Washing of the
Feet, the only two scenes without a landscape background and composed in
strict hieratic symmetry: they depict the two important readings for Maundy
Thursday.

PLATE 42

THE GOSPELS OF SAINT AUGUSTINE
fol. 129v *Luke*

Luke's Gospel is preceded by the portrait of the white-haired author, sitting in a frontal pose with crossed legs, his right arm raised to his chin in a gesture of meditation. All Evangelists ultimately derive from portraits of Greek philosophers and poets, but the type of this Luke is one of the rarest. While it has not survived in any Greek Evangelist portrait, it is known from an Armenian Gospel Book of Queen Mlke in Venice (generally dated 902 A.D.) which, like our portrait, is surely based on a Greek prototype. Luke is set against a niche with a portal, a reminder of the Porta Regia of the *scenae frons*. The four columns of colored marble in front of the niche, originally forming a tempietto, are, as in the Canon Tables, completely flattened and turned into a decorative frame. Differently stylized and abstracted, this type of setting ultimately goes back to the same root as the setting around Mark in the Rossano Gospels (Plate 33). However, the purely Western tradition asserts itself in the Evangelist's symbol, the protome of a winged bull, in the decoratively framed lunette.

The illustrator used the narrower outer intervals between the columns for scenes which, unlike the collective page (Plate 41), are not from a harmonized cycle but all from Luke's Gospel, beginning with the Annunciation at the upper left and ending with Zacchaeus in the fig tree at the lower right. Here, the illustrator goes even further in the process of condensation, squeezing two scenes into each of the six panels, thereby making the figures even more crowded and cut off by frame or hills.

The Italian artist has gone quite far in flattening the Evangelist figure and in replacing organic body structure by a system of curving lines, creating a pleasing pattern. Here the same tendencies to move away from the classical tradition are felt as in the *Vergilius Romanus* (Plates 12-14), but this artist has a greater sensitivity in his linear design.

PLATE 43

THE LONDON CANON TABLES
fol. 11r *Canon Table*

Perhaps the most precious fragments of any Early Christian manuscript are the
two leaves from a set of Canon Tables and the prefacing letter of Eusebius in
the British Library. Unfortunately, they were cut to fit into a twelfth-century
Gospel Book of smaller format. Even rarer than purple-stained leaves, these are
stained gold, forming a background for a lunette supported originally by three
columns forming two arches. The arches and columns are filled with an abstract
ornament consisting of stylized palmettes supported by omegas with pod-like
sides. The bright color of the ornament has an enamel-like quality, which is
effectively silhouetted against the gold. Because of this patternization, the architectural members, including the lace-like capitals, completely lose their struc-
tural sense. The closest parallels to these orientalizing patterns are found in
textile borders, which may have provided the actual inspiration.

Under each of the two arches is a portrait medallion, very classical in its realistic face and its free brush technique. There were originally twelve such medallions and they have correctly been interpreted as the twelve Apostles. Since
the Apostles have no direct connection with the concordances of the Canons
and the Eusebius letter, it has been suggested that they have an ultimate topo-
graphical origin, harking back to a set of *imagines clipeatae* that decorated the
interior of Constantine's mausoleum attached to the Apostle Church of Constantinople. Since we obviously are dealing with leaves of such extraordinary
splendor that their imperial patronage and Constantinopolitan origin can
rightly be assumed, the association with the Holy Apostles' Church has much to
recommend it. An origin at the end of the sixth or seventh century is most
likely.

PLATE 44

ASHBURNHAM PENTATEUCH
fol. 6r *Cain & Abel*

The thirteen verses from Genesis 3:21 to 4:9 are illustrated in one miniature
by no fewer than nine scenes which the illustrator distributed over the surface in
a purely decorative manner with utter disregard for the correct sequence. The
cycle starts properly at the upper left, with Adam and Eve under a bower, but
ends at the right of the second row, with the Lord questioning Cain. The nurs-
ing of Cain and Abel are separated and placed in two different registers, and
the scene of the brothers' sacrifices and their reception by the Lord are in
reversed order, to enumerate only two points of discrepancy.

A very striking effect is produced by the division of the picture into three
zones, each of a different color of strong emotional value against which the
figures, some in very dramatic poses, are silhouetted: a stirring, fiery orange at
the top, a pastural green in the middle, and a foreboding, gloomy purple at the
bottom. The lower zone is larger than the others: an arched area is reserved for
the most spectacular scene, the slaying of Abel by Cain; and in spandrel-like
areas Abel pastures his flocks, and Cain tills the soil with a team of bullocks. A
field of grain is placed at the lower right as a space-filler.

The strange motif of the bower with forked supports is found also in the
ninth-century Grandval Bible from Tours, which is iconographically based on
the Cotton Genesis. Yet although there may be some connections with this
Alexandrian Bible tradition, as a whole the Ashburnham Pentateuch does not
belong to this Egyptian picture recension but to some unknown center, not
impossibly North African, which developed its own style and iconography of
great character and expressiveness.

PLATE 45

ASHBURNHAM PENTATEUCH
fol. 9r *Deluge*

Giving special importance to the Deluge, the illustrator fills a full page with this single subject. The blue ark with red, pink, and brown stripes is of a very unusual shape, resembling more a chest resting on feet than a ship. In the water below, naturalistically colored a murky dark green, float two large and two small human corpses, dwarfing the floating horses and increasing the macabre effect. Since the *Midrashim* speak of "giants of so great stature and strength that the waters alone could not have made an end of them," it is indeed very probable that the Ashburnham Pentateuch has incorporated elements from Jewish tradition.

The macabre aspect also appears in some of the later richly illustrated Spanish Beatus–Apocalypse manuscripts. On the basis of such connections, some scholars have believed the Ashburnham Pentateuch itself to be a Spanish product. This is still an open question, although it is undeniable that, if not made in Spain proper, it exerted a strong influence on Spanish art.

The Deluge also takes a very prominent place in the Vienna Genesis (Plate 23), but here its composition, depicting the actual rainfall and some struggling victims, is very different. The Deluge scene in the Cotton Genesis, preserved only in the mosaic copy of San Marco in Venice, is also very different. This is all the more noteworthy since, in the previous miniature, some relations to the Cotton Genesis recension were noticed. Among the Early Christian representations of this subject, the miniature in the Ashburnham Pentateuch remains unique.

QUIUENI PERAGRUMINOCCUR
SUMNOBIS DIXITQ·ELIPSEEST
DOLINA IS MEUS·ATILLA TOLLENS
CITO PALLIUMOPERUITSE· SER
UUSAUTEMCUNCTAQUAEGES
SERATNARRAUIT·ISAAC

XXVI· QUIIN TRODUXITEAM INTABERNA
CULUMSARRAEMATRIS SUAE
EIACCEPITEAMUXOREM· ETINTAN
TUMDILEXIT·UTDOLOREM·QUIEX
MORTEMATRISACCIDERAT·
TEMPERARET

46

47

PLATE 46

A S H B U R N H A M   P E N T A T E U C H
fol. 21r   *Isaac & Rebecca*

The scenes covering the episode of Rebecca at the well are once more distributed over the surface out of order, beginning with Eliezer, Abraham's servant,
seated contemplatively at the well at the right of the middle register. Rebecca
approaches with a water jar over her shoulder in the very center of the picture,
separated from him by a scene in which she has just drawn water from the well
to give Eliezer a drink. At the same time, he puts a ring on her finger. Here,
clearly, two actions are conflated which originally were rendered in two separate scenes—proof that an even richer cycle was used as a model. How different
are these scenes, the surface densely filled with disregard of spatial relationships, from the parallel ones in the Vienna Genesis, where simply dressed classical figures move freely in open space (Plate 24).

Compared with earlier, concise Bible illustration, there is in the subsequent
scenes a tendency to expand and to create grand settings. The reception of Eliezer in Laban's house, at the top of the page, is placed in the country villa of a
rich landowner such as one sees in Tunisian floor mosaics, but in the miniature
the disconnected parts form a fantastic ensemble. This kind of setting is
repeated at the lower right, where Rebecca is introduced to Isaac in the presence of old Abraham. Moreover, emphasis is particularly placed on the com-
plete visibility of each of the ten camels in the upper scene, and on a group of
servants, including some black ones. Luxuriousness is displayed in the richly
embroidered garment and headdress of Rebecca. The biblical narrative is
almost hidden in these extraneous addenda, which are colorful and lively and
exhibit a quality peculiar to the Ashburnham Pentateuch and unparalleled by
any other known manuscript.

PLATE 47

ASHBURNHAM PENTATEUCH
fol. 76r   *Moses Receiving Law*

Some of the pictures for Exodus do not follow the Bible text as closely as those for Genesis. The upper half of a miniature showing Moses at Sinai still has a narrative character, but with changes and additions. Moses has gone up the mountain, leaving Aaron and his sons Nadab and Abihu behind (Exodus 22:1ff.). He is talking to the Lord, whose face appears in a cloud, a feature incorporated from chapter 19. From the mountain range, as craggy as it is in reality, shoot high flames, and the powerful dynamism of the scene is increased by their breaking through the upper frame. Below, Moses reads from the tablets to a large crowd of Israelites, men and festively dressed women, standing behind an altar which he has erected to receive a burnt offering. But instead of sacrificial oxen, one notices on the altar a chalice and breads, clearly a prefiguration of the Christian eucharist.

The lower half has no visible association with any biblical passage. The desert tents with Aaron and Joshua at the left and Aaron and his sons at the right are clearly pushed aside to give way to an elaborate representation of the tabernacle in the form of a temple. The exchange of the constructed temple for the desert tabernacle may well go back to a Jewish source.

The juxtaposition of Moses climbing the mountain at the top and a more static scene with the temple-tabernacle below is also found in the Carolingian Bibles made at Tours, and there is indeed a likelihood of a common archetype. It is fitting that we should leave the last biblical scene we have described with a question mark, reminding the reader of the extreme scarcity of evidence, which does not permit us to trace the influence of illustrated Bibles within ecumenical Christianity in all its details.

PLATE 48

CODEX AMIATINUS
fol. Vr *Ezra*

It was quite likely Cassiodorus' idea to preface the Codex Grandior, one of the Bibles copied at Vivarium in Calabria, by a portrait of Ezra, the prophet and scribe who rewrote the Holy Scripture after the end of the Babylonian captivity. The choice may well have been made as an allusion to Cassiodorus' own activity as a scribe. The traditional portrait of Ezra in Bible illustration, like that of all Prophets, was a standing figure, and so he is depicted in the Syrian Bible of Paris (Figure XII). But in the Codex Amiatinus a Byzantine Evangelist, writing busily in a large codex held on his knees, was used as a model and adjusted by placing a tallith on his head and a plate with twelve stones before his breast. The cupboard, which has leatherbound books, presumably Bibles, on its shelves, also goes back to an early tradition when the shelves were still filled with scrolls.

About 700 A.D. the Codex Grandior must have been at Jarrow-Wearmouth where the Amiatinus copy was made. It is still debated whether the Ezra picture was made by an Italian artist working in the Northumbrian monastery or by a native Anglo-Saxon. In support of the first alternative is Ezra's closeness to the Byzantine Evangelist type, his pose, drapery, the furniture and the writing paraphernalia, and the miniature's stylistic affinity to Roman frescoes from the end of the seventh century. Among the factors favouring the second is the decorative use of color in the garments, whereby the red mantle becomes in its lower part the tunic, and the green tunic the mantle.

CODICIBVS SACRIS HOSTILI CLADE PERVSTIS

ESDRA DŌ FERVENS HOC REPARAVIT OPVS

48